Rivers
OF
Cornwall

SARAH FOOT

BOSSINEY BOOKS

First published in 1984
by Bossiney Books
St Teath, Bodmin, Cornwall.
Designed, printed and bound in Great Britain by
A. Wheaton & Co, Exeter.

© Sarah Foot 1984
ISBN   0 906456 91 6

Plate Acknowledgments

Front cover by Ray Bishop
Back cover by Alice Boyd
Pages 3, 4, 6–9, 10, 12, 16–23, 26–38, 42, 43,
45–54, 56–60, 64, 86–88, 92, 93–98, 102, 106, 107,
112, 115, 118, 119 Ray Bishop
Pages 5, 11, 13, 55, 61–63, 66–72, 74 lower, 76–81,
100, 101, 104, 105, 109, 113 Alice Boyd
Pages 15, 24, 25, 40, 41, 65, 110, 111, 116, 117 Mike
Frost
Pages 14, 90, 91, 99 Peter Keeling
Page 44 Margaret Rowe
Page 39 John Watts
Page 89 Jim Morrison
Page 8 Ken Duxbury
Page 108 Natalie Allen
Page 103 Roseanne Foot
Page 114 Mary Martin

ABOUT THE AUTHOR AND THE BOOK

Sarah Foot lives in a beautiful converted barn at Elmgate, overlooking the River Lynher. Formerly on the staff of *The London Evening News*, she contributes regularly to *The Western Morning News*. This is her eighth title for Bossiney, her seventh being *The Cornish Countryside*, Bossiney's first venture in combining colour and black and white photography which was featured on both Television South West and Channel Four.

In 1981 she wrote the text for *Views of Old Cornwall*, a collection of Victorian and Edwardian picture postcards, and followed it with *Views of Old Plymouth* in the Spring of 1983. Her other Bossiney titles are *A Cornish Camera*, in collaboration with photographer George Ellis, *My Grandfather Isaac Foot*, which was the subject of a BBC TV tie-in, *Following the Tamar* and *Following the River Fowey*.

Here in *Rivers of Cornwall* Sarah Foot, accompanied by talented photographers, explores six great Cornish rivers: the Helford, the Fal, the Fowey, the Camel, the Lynher, and the Tamar. 'I have become excited, exhilarated, surprised and often "mazed"—as the Cornish say—when following these famous rivers, and discovering the stories they have to tell.' As the author perceptively reflects: 'It is the rivers which connect the great variety and brilliance of the countryside. As I have gone out to discover the stories of these rivers, I have been enthralled again and again by the differences, within a few miles, of landscape and people.'

The Author with Bill Lindsey on the ferry at Padstow.

Rivers of Cornwall

Rivers are the great link between countryside and sea. Travelling as they do from moor or bog down to the coast, they embrace a great variety of scenery and by following their courses we can discover a wealth of stories, legends, history and modern lifestyles.

Flowing through farm and woodland, past mills, over huge boulders and under ancient stone bridges, they lend at all times a special quality to the landscape.

It is not surprising that the hidden charm of the river valleys has captivated many a writer, painter and lover of wildlife, and the men who have lived and worked by the rivers—boatbuilders, fishermen, millers and water bailiffs—are staunch protectors of the rivers' beauties and importance.

There are many rivers in Cornwall but I have chosen just six: the Tamar, the Lynher, the Fowey, the Camel, the Helford and the Fal. They are some of the finest, most interesting rivers anyone could hope to find. I have become excited, exhilarated, surprised and often 'mazed'—as the Cornish say—when following these famous rivers and hearing the stories they have to tell.

John Norden who wrote an historical survey of Cornwall in the sixteenth century said of the rivers of

Cornish rivers 'lend a special quality to the landscape'. Left: The Author in Frenchman's Creek. Right: The River Lynher near Trebartha.

Cornwall: 'There are within Cornwall some rivers, as Tamar, Loo and Foy. But of brookes and pills there are infinite, that flow from sweete and pleasant springs, that rise among the montaynes and rocks; a necessarie helpe to the mountainous cattle and often times to wayfaring travellors. There are manie small coves and creeks and harbors and small boates, especially on the south coast; where are also the principle havens of Loo, Foy, Helford and Falmouth.'

These comments about river life in Cornwall written almost exactly four hundred years ago still hold true, although life on the rivers has changed and changed again.

The estuaries of Cornwall's rivers are grand and beautiful and the havens that Norden wrote about still exist. Along the estuaries there is a multitude of wildlife, particularly birds, to be seen and enjoyed.

Once great sailing ships made their way miles up these rivers to Lostwithiel on the Fowey, Wadebridge on the Camel, Morwellham on the Tamar, Notter Bridge on the Lynher, Tregony on the Fal and Gweek on the Helford. Now, some of the rivers have silted up and the boats one sees are no longer the working tugs, schooners and barges of earlier times, but more often the modern pleasure craft of a more leisured people.

Two views of the Helford River: '. . . each river holds its own atmosphere.'

Before there were proper roads or railways all industrial cargoes, farm produce and fertilisers were transported by river. Stone and tin, copper and coal, lime for improving the land, as well as barley, wheat and maize, were all conveyed by water. Owning a boat meant being able to earn a living and this only changed when the railways came.

It is not surprising that such writers and artists as Turner, Thomas Rowlandson, Tennyson, W. E. Grahame, Daphne du Maurier, Sir Arthur Quiller Couch, Sir John Betjeman and many others came to create their pictures, stories, poems and sometimes their homes along the rivers of Cornwall.

Each river has its own character, and whereas the jagged coastline is synonymous with much that is flinty in the Cornish character, so the secret and protected valleys are alike to another side of the Cornish people: they too often hide what is best in them.

I was brought up on the banks of the River Lynher and so, like all those with happy childhood memories, I remember this backdrop to my early years as one of the most beautiful places in the world.

I then came to love the Fowey when I followed it from the source on Bodmin Moor down to the haven of Fowey town. Later I lived by the Tamar and realised that the history and community feeling in that valley is unparalleled and the atmosphere of a tightly knit fellowship exists even today when the activities that take place on the slopes have changed so much.

The Helford and the Fal are alike in many ways and the people who have worked these rivers in barges and sailing ships often know both rivers equally well. Here there are still men who made their living from the river traffic. The days of the working boats that carried goods inland from the harbour of Falmouth have almost gone, but are still in living memory. The oyster dredging under sail, however, still survives, even though on a much smaller scale than it once did.

In Falmouth I found that people are often known by the kind of boat they owned or worked. Sailing boats are talked about by name as if they were living and breathing things: some had more reliable facets than others, some were more adventurous, others more beautiful, some were tragic. The owners relied on their boats for their importance in life.

The Roseland countryside that runs along the eastern side of the Fal is believed to be some of the loveliest in Cornwall, and discovering it for the first

Left: Sailing at the mouth of the Camel estuary. Right: Lobster pots on the quay at Padstow.

8

time when researching this book I felt as if I had found a whole new world.

As I wandered along these river banks and talked to some of the people who live there, I came to realise that each river holds its own atmosphere. I have also begun to understand that a river can affect people's lives and become almost an obsession. Like every part of the Cornish landscape the river banks owe much of their character to their ancient history. So much in Cornwall has stayed unchanged as the people held

out against those who wanted to alter their land. This stand against change is still an intricate part of the Cornish character. They had to fight against invaders, were suspicious of foreigners, and proud of their heritage and independence, and so they remain today.

Perhaps it is significant that some of the most popular settlers, and some of the first, were the Celtic saints, the holy men and women who came from Ireland, Wales and Brittany. They did not come to force their ideas, or to disrupt the community. They moved into small hermitages slightly apart from other settlements, and only gradually imparted their Christian beliefs in an aloof yet loving way.

Some of the most outstanding beauty spots, therefore, on many Cornish rivers were first found and inhabited by these Celtic saints. On ancient granite pagan stones they marked their sign of the Christian cross, they gently influenced the barbaric ways of the men who had come before them and were anxious to offer a form of education to all people. Above all they did not patronise, behaviour Cornish people cannot abide.

You will find, for instance, at Halton Quay on the Tamar and at St Winnow on the Fowey, holy places with an atmosphere so peaceful it would be impossible not to feel the healing powers. These were originally Celtic holy places.

The slow rate of change has kept alive this hallowed feeling in much of Cornwall, but the rivers were also working places and they have known a busy, active, and sometimes hard, life too.

You can enter the whole world of Cornish history if you follow the rivers. Visiting churches and chapels you learn not only of those hundreds of Celtic saints—there are more in Cornwall than there are in Heaven, they say—but also of the names and occupations of the families who lived in the area, of the sudden deaths and long lives, and of the changes brought about by the Reformation and the Civil War.

You will discover river crossings where the King's men met with Cromwell's men and on the hill forts hear of ancient legends of King Arthur, Tristan and Iseult. In the havens you will see the castles and blockhouses built to keep out the French and Dutch and Spanish. In the little creeks and pills stories are still told of smugglers and reckless privateers. Here,

*Cornish rivers were busy with traffic and
activity.   Left: Hingham Mill on a tributary of
the River Camel.   Below: The railway viaduct
at Antony passage.*

too, you will find evidence of the travels of John Wesley and his brother who, through their preaching, became the great spiritual liberators of the miners, fishermen and farmers of the area.

Facts and dates intermingle. It sometimes seems quite impossible to put Cornish history into sequence and I am sure this is because Cornish people have a genius for keeping their history alive, talking about the stories of five hundred years ago as if they happened in living memory.

People will tell you where a Celtic saint landed as if

they saw it with their own eyes, and show you the spot in the river where the last King of Cornwall drowned. In the same breath they describe the behaviour of the Parliamentarians, point out old lime kilns and where they themselves worked alongside barge quays and water mills. Which came first or last does not seem to matter, but that these things happened at all is of paramount importance.

Some say, for instance, that King Arthur never existed, or if he did he never came to Cornwall. But up along the banks of the Camel you will find people who are perfectly certain he was there, hunted on the moors, walked and talked with his gallant knights, and that he will return when the Cornish chough flies once more over the Cornish cliffs.

Giants' steps and stones, Devil's jumps, saints' hermitages and chapels, kings' mansions, smuggling inns, working water mills, derelict but once busy quays, mine houses, boatbuilding yards, are all part of river life. Sadly many of the old, once busy riverside towns and villages are now taken over by cottages, empty during the winter months, rented out to visitors in the summer, but some of the communities remain to keep alive and relate the river life.

It is the rivers which connect the great variety and brilliance of the countryside. As I have gone out to discover the stories of these rivers, I have been enthralled again and again by the differences, within a few miles, of landscape and people.

Down through wooded valleys you will suddenly find wide open water-meadows, rise again to the bare earth of moorland, then find still pools or rushing waterfalls where huge boulders change the water's course. Always there is the marvel of coming to the end of the river and seeing its expulsion to the open sea.

Kenneth Grahame, who spent a great deal of time on the Fowey River, described it all beautifully in that chapter of *Wind in the Willows* when Mole feels the call of spring and discovers a river. 'Never in his life had he seen a river before—this sleek sinuous, full

Low tide on the River Camel.

12

Spring on the Lynher.

The peacefulness of the Fal. The Drake Fellowship sailing barge Lady Daphne *pictured at first light off Turnaware Point.*

Dunlin are winter visitors to our estuaries where large numbers can be seen feeding on the mudflats. In the past it has bred on Bodmin Moor.

bodied animal . . . The mole was bewitched, entranced, fascinated. By the side of the river he trotted as one trots when very small, by the side of a man who holds one spell-bound by exciting stories; and when tired at last, he sat on the bank while the river still chattered on to him, a babbling procession of the best stories in the world sent from the heart of the earth to be told at last to the insatiable sea.'

Here, in words and pictures, are just some of the 'best stories in the world sent from the heart of the earth'; they come from six of the most fascinating and beautiful rivers of Cornwall. I hope they will remind some people of old stories now forgotten or inform others for the first time of the rich diversity of life and scenery which exists along the banks of our Cornish rivers.

The Helford River

The Helford River has suffered something of an invasion along its banks. Newcomers have, in many cases, replaced the indigenous population. I was told there are no Cornish people living at Helford Passage, and on the other side of the river at Helford itself I found only one Cornish family still residing there. Yet it remains a mysterious and often haunting stretch of water.

You can understand, if you walk along the banks of the famous Frenchman's Creek, why and how Daphne du Maurier's imagination took flight in these lonely, tree-lined creeks, and developed into the evocative story for her famous novel of the same name.

At Port Navas, centre of the oyster industry, you may see large and luxurious vessels moored but it does not eliminate the feeling that once such little harbours as this were hiding places for privateers and smugglers. The new houses built above the river may be of modern and lavish design and yet, hanging in the air, is the feeling of some mystery that has managed to outlive the modern development.

Some Cornish people, ousted by rising rates and rents and lack of trade, resent this intrusion into their lives which were once private and comparatively untouched by the outside world, but one must not forget that the newcomers to the River Helford have a right to love and cherish the place too. They have often come from busy cities in search of a better quality of life, and they have found it here.

In the summer the villages and harbours along the

The Helford is the hidden river.   Left: Lonely tree-lined Frenchman's Creek.   Right: The Helford meets the sea beyond Durgan.

The Woods of Calamansack: '. . . just one of the Helford names with a musical ring.'

This sailing barge moored at Gweek recalls the once-thriving port.

Helford are full of people; visitors come in their droves to wander along the river and rent houses and flats which often lie empty in the winter months. They change the atmosphere a little, but those who live there through the winter and the misty days of autumn, treat the summer visitors with forbearance and wait until this precious land is returned to them. Some of them remain in their houses amongst the woods, not venturing out, guarding their privacy with a vengeance.

Once the summer months are over, the seasonal houses empty, many of the lights go out. There is a quiet that returns to the river and the creeks and harbours and the Helford belongs once again to those who love and live along its banks through all the seasons, lights and climates.

No-one could have loved the Helford or understood its secrets and its beauties better than C. C. Vyvyan, who wrote a book entitled *The Helford River* just after the war. She lived with her husband Sir Courtnay Vyvyan at the great house of Trelowarren and worked with him to keep house and gardens in a good state of repair. She roamed on foot and by rowing boat along every part of the Helford River from Gweek down to the sea.

People still remember her as she wandered through the lanes in her coloured stockings and jerseys, often walking home to Trelowarren from a friend's house in the moonlight. Over the forty years that she lived by the river she came to know everyone and every nook and cranny of the place and her relationship with the river became a great love affair.

In 1941 her husband died and after the war Lady Vyvyan worked hard to establish a market garden in the grounds, in which she toiled herself. Her love for the house and estate was always closely linked with the river which she said drew everyone like a magnet.

The Vyvyan family have lived at Trelowarren for over 500 years. The house, with its adjoining chapel, and its grounds rising from the hollow in which the house is so protected, is a beautiful place and now open to the public. The Cornish Crafts Association holds its annual exhibition there and was visited in April 1979 by Prince Charles who has shown a keen interest in the work of Cornish craftsmen. There is

Helford: 'There is a quiet that returns to the river and the creeks . . .'

also a camping site in the grounds and a fine walk through National Trust woods to Tremayne quay.

It is all greatly changed since the peaceful days when Lady Vyvyan lived and worked at the house. The sanctuary she so loved has had to be opened up to many activities and people so that it can survive in a modern world. Yet when you visit Trelowarren, if you have ever read her books about her gardening years as well as her story of the river, you can feel the spell it cast on her.

According to her book there are twenty or thirty streams, brooks and rivulets which feed the River Helford and she should know for one of her favourite pastimes was to go in search of the streams, sometimes through almost impenetrable undergrowth, and follow them, in gum boots and bearing a strong stick, as far as she could.

The main part of the river runs between the old harbour at Gweek down to the sea beyond Dennis Head and Toll Point. Gweek was once a flourishing harbour full of sailing ships bringing up their cargoes of coal, cement, wood, grain and limestone. Boats came from all over the Continent and Ireland, and Gweek was a thriving port serving the town of Helston as well as villages and hamlets further down river. Timber came in large quantities, the great trunks often being poled up the last reaches of the river and then lying in a large mass below the bridge.

If you go to Gweek now there is still a sense of all that has gone before. You feel that this is a place where men worked hard, where risks were taken and deals made. I remembered Jim Morrison, the working boatman of Falmouth, telling me of the days when he did a lot of business at Gweek, relying on his canny knowledge of tides and channels to deliver safely and return to Falmouth.

There is still an old masted sailing boat moored at Gweek and some boatbuilders at work, but Gweek is probably as well known for its Seal Sanctuary as anything else.

The sanctuary has done marvellous work in saving, nurturing, and sometimes returning to the sea, seals

When you visit Trelowarren (left) – home of the Vyvyan family for 500 years – you can still feel the spell the house and river cast on Lady Vyvyan. In gum boots and bearing a strong stick she went in search of stream, brook and rivulet.   Above: The Helford near Gweek.

At Durgan on the Helford –
a visit will never disappoint.

who have been injured, often by man's carelessness or misuse of the elements. Ken and Mary Jones have become famous for the work they have carried out in the well-designed and unobtrusive sanctuary, and have made it into a going concern by opening it to visitors. They have also done much to educate people about the life and ways of these most appealing creatures.

From Gweek you can take the north or south road to follow the river, either drive will take you to unforgettable places. To the north lies the road to Constantine, Port Navas, Durgan and Mawnan, and the woods and farm of Calamansack.

Ever since I read Quiller Couch's poem I had a longing to see this wooded piece of the Helford which he wrote about so charmingly.

All the wood to ransack
All the wave explore
Moon on Calamansack,
Ripple on the shore.
Laid asleep and dreaming
On our cabin beds;
Helford River streaming
By two happy heads.

Two aspects of Helford Passage – from here a passenger ferry runs across the river to Helford.

Calamansack is just one of the Helford names with a musical ring. It was C. C. Vyvyan again who recited in her book a marvellous string of names nearby: 'All day and every day, all night and every night', she wrote, 'the river receives water, his own life blood, flowing down to him from the homes and hamlets of Traboe, Trewince, Tregevas, Lean Caervallock, Carabone, Billy, Meanlay, Chygarkye, Treverry, Zula, Nancemerrin, Mellangoose, Treloquithack, Boswidjack, Carwythenack, Treworvack and Treviades.'

Wonderful names, conjuring up so many feelings, and each one of them a part of the history of the area.

One bright May day I walked with Ray Bishop, who took many of the photographs for this book, down the steep lane to Durgan.

There was something particular in the light that day. Clear, bright and sharp, yet with an unusual warmth, a light that only comes in the first days of

children splashing about in the surprisingly warm water.

The sun glazed the aquamarine water, movements were gentle and slow, the shouts of children were not offensive but subdued. There was a happiness as if the first strong sun proclaimed a new birth. Some hikers appeared from the path that leads down to Durgan from the gardens of the house of Glendurgan above and complained that it was too hot to walk.

I shall never forget that day as we stood at the bottom of the slope, having walked down the shady lane, and admired that scene like some from a children's picture book.

Once most of the buildings at Durgan belonged to the fishermen, and most of the fishermen had donkeys which were led, with their panniers full of fish, five miles to Falmouth market by the fishermen's wives. The donkeys were allowed to roam free in the lanes when they were not hard at work and it was a familiar sight to see them around the area, grazing happily where they could. Occasionally they would be impounded in a field, kept specially for the purpose, until their owners came to collect them.

The Fox family have owned the house of Glendurgan for over a hundred years. For three centuries the early generations of this family were Quakers and very keen gardeners. The first Fox to come to Cornwall was Francis Fox who lived in the parish of St Germans in the seventeenth century. His descendants moved to Fowey and then in 1759 to Falmouth where they started their well-known business as shipping and travel agents.

The gardens of Glendurgan are now owned by the National Trust and are open three days a week. They were originally planted by Alfred Fox in the 1820s and 1830s. On the gate posts leading into the gardens are two little statues of foxes, to remind us of the family association. The garden is famous for its many rare shrubs and the maze of laurel bushes which was planted in 1833.

The Pound House at Glendurgan was the first day

summer, a light that does not often show itself for more than a few days each year.

It was the half-term school holiday, and the little harbour beneath the pine trees, spreading out from the grey housed hamlet, was littered with boats of every size and with the cheerful cries of happy

Estuaries and rivers throughout Cornwall are graced by the presence of the mute swan.

school in Mawnan Parish and was built by Alfred Fox in the 1820s for the education of the Durgan children. The first teacher there was Alfred Fox's wife, Sarah.

A visit to Glendurgan and the hamlet of Durgan below will never disappoint, and since the National Trust have opened a carpark above the village, where all is quiet and picturesque enough for picnics, the narrow lane down to the river is unspoilt by traffic and makes an exciting walk if rather steep.

If, then, Port Navas, Durgan and Helford Passage on the north side of the river are all unique places with wonderful views so is the south side just as picturesque, if not more so.

I never fail to love the drive from Gweek along this south side of the river, sometimes perched high above amongst the trees, sometimes coming down to cross rivulets and creeks. A large part belonged to the Vyvyan family of Trelowarren and it would be

Farmland, woods and estuary come together at Helford.

wrong to pass along this road without visiting the house and paying one's respects to the place where past masters kept alive the best of the feudal system.

To walk along Frenchman's Creek or Pill, as it is more often called by the local people, is a treat in store for anyone who has never ventured there. The first time I went it was early spring. Primroses carpeted the banks of the pathway. The trees were not yet in leaf, but buds were promising great changes in the landscape. I walked with two friends—we stayed silent—and I noticed the few people we passed did not speak either; we smiled at each other in greeting. There is a quietness to the place that it would be a crime to shatter. The tide was in that day and some dead trees lay collapsed into the water. We climbed out onto the trunk of one of these trees and sat there over the water and looked down the river towards Helford. It is easy to believe that there is a door that shuts this place off from the rest of the world, that you are in undiscovered land. That afternoon we sat and drank in the peacefulness and felt, with renewed conviction, that the world was a wonderful place.

Driving down the steep slope to Helford village in winter you may feel that this is a lost and forgotten land. A few villagers walk to and fro, the thatched houses cluster around the inlet of water, curtains are drawn in many of the houses, their residents only part-time dwellers. Yet there is still a community feeling here, though many of the inmates are relative newcomers.

Rob and Angela Smith took over the village shop and post office in 1983 from Chris Blount of Radio Cornwall. They have become popular members of the village community with their two young children. They are an attractive and lively couple who left the hurly burly of a London job and commuter living in Reigate to find a more rewarding way of life. They reckon they have achieved that ambition.

Rob keeps a sailing boat and very kindly offered to take me up river one sunny day. At a time when the weather was being most unpredictable we found a marvellously clear day in an otherwise rainy week. It is wonderful to set out from Helford, join the wider part of the river and gently make your way upstream

Port Navas – yachtsman's paradise and home of the Duchy of Cornwall oyster farm.

towards Frenchman's Creek. What struck me most about the experience is how different it is to see places from the water.

As soon as we reached Frenchman's Creek, I felt we were entering a part of the river that was out of bounds. We were intruders. This day the trees were in full leaf and it felt as if they might enclose us, take a hold and never let us return to the outside world. It is a haunting melancholy feeling, and I would not like to have been there on my own. There is something exciting and unique about this creek; it makes one wonder what on earth has gone on there before to leave such sadness on the water, and yet on the banks I had felt only peacefulness. Rob Smith told me that many people feel that Frenchman's Creek is 'spooked' and are afraid to sail there.

Coming out of the creek proved something of a relief and it was fine to look across at Calamansack and Helford Passage and then cross the river and visit Port Navas.

Up above the harbour of Port Navas I could see

27

Working and pleasure boats on the Helford:
'. . . for generations men have found wind and
sea irresistible.'

Len Hodges' house where he once took me unannounced to lunch. His organised and cheerful wife welcomed me warmly and gave me a delicious meal only equalled by the view and situation of their home.

Len has been running the Oyster Farm at Port Navas for many years; his father ran it before him and his son hopes to run it after him. But this is a sad time for the oyster business since a disease, which may have been brought from abroad, has spread like wild fire and destroyed many of the oysters. It will be a tragedy if this does put a stop to oyster fishing in the area for it has been carried on in the Helford River for over 2,000 years. Oyster fishing has kept genuine working people in the vicinity, something that is vitally needed along the banks of the Helford, for without working people a place eventually loses its character and its reason for being.

Back in Helford, after our perfect boat trip, I felt sad to be on dry land—visiting places by boat gives a whole new dimension to all rivers—but I was determined to talk to Emmie Hewett, the last Cornishwoman to live in Helford. Even she will be gone soon to live in Manaccan.

Emmie was born in Helford and has lived in her present house ever since she married her husband Frank who worked as a foreman electrician at Culdrose. They have happily lived there for forty years and Emmie runs a tea garden which is always full to overflowing in the summer months. Sadly she now has bad arthritis and cannot manage the steep slopes

Magical light on the river at The Shipwright Arms, Helford.

which lead to her terraced garden where the little tables are laid out for cream teas every sunny day.

She told me that in the winter months, when the sun has gone down, there are few lights to be seen in the houses around. Many of them are deserted and she feels that it is sad, and a different place from when she first came as a bride.

Now the fishermen who keep their boats at Helford are often men from Cadgwith, Lizard or St Keverne, none of them living in Helford anymore.

The Riverside Inn at Helford is a restaurant open from March to October with an international reputation for fine food and it is this restaurant which has brought people from all over the world to the village. The food and accommodation, though expensive, are of an extremely high standard and people say those who stay at the Riverside or go there for a meal will talk of the experience for sometime after. The locals admire the place, speak of it with a certain amount of pride, but are not likely to frequent it.

It was in March that I drove from Helford to the hamlet of St Anthony. I sat behind the little church in the sloping graveyard and looked out at the boats beyond in the harbour. In the bay there were some young men wind surfing and I thought how for

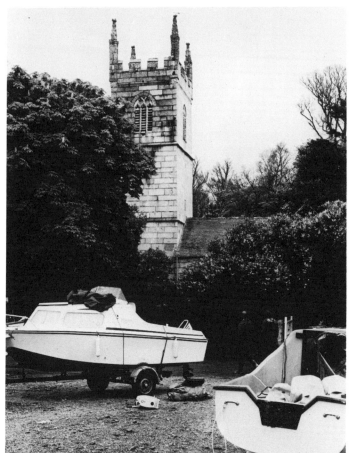

Left: Emmie Hewett, the last Cornishwoman living in Helford (right). Above: St Anthony Church built, so the legend goes, by shipwrecked Normans.

generations men have found wind and sea irresistible elements with which to grapple and attempt to master.

St Anthony, Manaccan, St Martin, St Mawgan and St Keverne make up that part of the Lizard Peninsula which is known as Meneage or 'land of the monks'.

Legend tells us that the Church of St Anthony was built by a group of shipwrecked Normans who were caught in a storm while crossing from France to Cornwall. Their promise was that if they were saved they would build a church as thanksgiving. It is a legend that could be based on truth because the tower of the church is built from a fine granite apparently never found in Cornwall but quite common in Normandy. At any rate it seems fitting that the beginning of the church's life should be linked with the sea, for this is nearly the end of the Helford River. Beyond is the headland known as Dennis Head—from *dinas* meaning fortress.

At the fortress Sir Rickjard Vyvyan fought against the Parliamentarians during the Civil War and held out for several days against terrible odds. Not the first or last time that a Vyvyan has fought to protect the river banks as he thought fit. Other Vyvyans had gained a reputation for bravery when they were governors of St Mawes Castle at the entrance to the Fal.

Driving home from the River Helford I have thought so many times of its many-faceted character, wondering to myself which was the most typical. Was it the eerie Frenchman's Creek? Was it Port Navas or Durgan? Was it the way the river seems to hide away so much that is best? But what remained to impress me most was the way the mystery, the haunting mood of the river has not changed at all in spite of every kind of modern invasion. The mystery, we can be sure, will not be wiped out.

The Camel River

People say that nowhere in Cornwall can you be made to feel so much a foreigner as you can in Padstow. It was lucky for me, then, that when I started my exploration of the River Camel at its mouth and went to the harbour town of Padstow I found a friend in Bill Lindsey.

Bill is well known in Padstow. He has worked there since he was fourteen years old. He is now seventy eight. He is part of the place, knows everything that is going on, who is who and what happened when. Though he was able to give me an open passport to the town, he himself is still not considered a Padstonian. He was born in Wadebridge, and no amount of years living and working in Padstow can change the fact that he is a Wadebridger.

It does not seem to perturb him in the least, for he has done well in Padstow. Having worked from 1922 to 1945 in the boatbuilding trade, for many years in Brabyn's yard, he then took over the lease of the ferry which runs from Padstow to Rock on the opposite shore of the estuary several times every day, come rain or shine.

The ferry crossing, originally called Black Rock Passage, is a very ancient one and has existed for at least six hundred years. It has always belonged to the Duchy of Cornwall and having the lease of the ferry and being responsible for running it is considered to be quite a feather in any man's cap.

On the day Bill walked with me through the little streets of Padstow we went at a fast pace. 'You'd never think I had two new hips,' he said to me proudly. On the way there were the inevitable stops to greet old friends and neighbours. One such friend we visited was Margaret Rowe who runs an excellent book shop with many valuable old books amongst her collection, particularly volumes concerning Cornish history.

Her daughter, Patricia Bate, who works with her is an expert on second-hand books and knows almost anything you could wish to know about the world of literature and publishers. One could spend hours in the company of these women, leafing through the old books and talking to them of Padstow customs past and present.

Richard Carew of Antony, who wrote the famous *Survey of Cornwall* in the seventeenth century, spoke of the 'good fellowship of Padstow', and the allegiance to the town by those who are born and bred there is very strong. On May Day the ancient custom of the 'Obby 'Oss dance is re-enacted and those Padstonians living in exile return from wherever they are, whenever they can, for the great occasion.

It is an ancient rite, some parts of the festival going back to pagan times. The man who takes the part of the 'Obby 'Oss dances with great rhythm dressed

Padstow Harbour, one of few refuges on this treacherous north coast.

Margaret Rowe who runs the Strand Bookshop in Padstow.

over all in tarred sack cloth, all hooped and reaching to the ground and topped with a frightening mask. The Teaser entices him to dance and the procession, consisting of other dancers, singers and musicians, wends its way through the narrow streets of Padstow stopping at houses and shops and also visiting the great house of Prideaux Place.

Prideaux Place has been the home of the Prideaux family ever since the land was confiscated from the monasteries by Henry VIII and given to the family

who built the house. It is one of the few manor houses in Cornwall still lived in by the family who built it.

Although it is part of the town, built just above the twisting streets, it has its own deer park. Legend says that when the deer leave the park the family will also leave their old home.

I was lucky enough to see the 'Obby 'Oss procession this year on its visit to Prideaux Place and I don't know when I have last been so affected by music and dancing that seemed to throb through one's whole body. The melancholy dirge of the song, the intense rhythm of the drums is all-encompassing and the dexterity of the dancing is full of enthusiasm and skill.

A friend of mine, in recent years, went to follow the Padstow 'Obby 'Oss through the streets on May Day. She stayed with the procession all day long, for the celebrations last from dawn to way after dusk, and she told me that she could feel the beat of the music resounding through her body for days after the event. It is an intoxicating performance and one can see why it has meant so much to so many people, and remains such an enticement for a return home to those who have had to leave Padstow to work and live elsewhere.

Although the ancient festival of the 'Obby 'Oss is to do with the coming of spring and summer and fertility rites, it is also a declaration of a steadfastness amongst the community which is the core of the town of Padstow.

For many years David Farquhar, Margaret Rowe's brother, took the role of the 'Obby 'Oss and kept the custom going through the war years when many of the strong young men capable of keeping up the ritual were away. He is another character closely connected with the ferry and was active in setting up the Padstow Museum, a little gem of a place full of fascinating items of interest from the history of the town.

On the day Bill Lindsey led me around Padstow he promised to ride with me on the ferry. He does not need to buy a ticket and would be most put out if anyone asked him to, for he still retains the honorary title of Ferryman of Padstow.

It was a beautiful sunny day, all the shops were just

Prideaux Place: '. . . one of the few manor houses in Cornwall still lived in by the family who built it.'

'As we boarded the ferry boat Bill Lindsey
introduced me to the ferryman, Peter McBurnie,
whose father worked on the ferry with Bill for
nine years.'

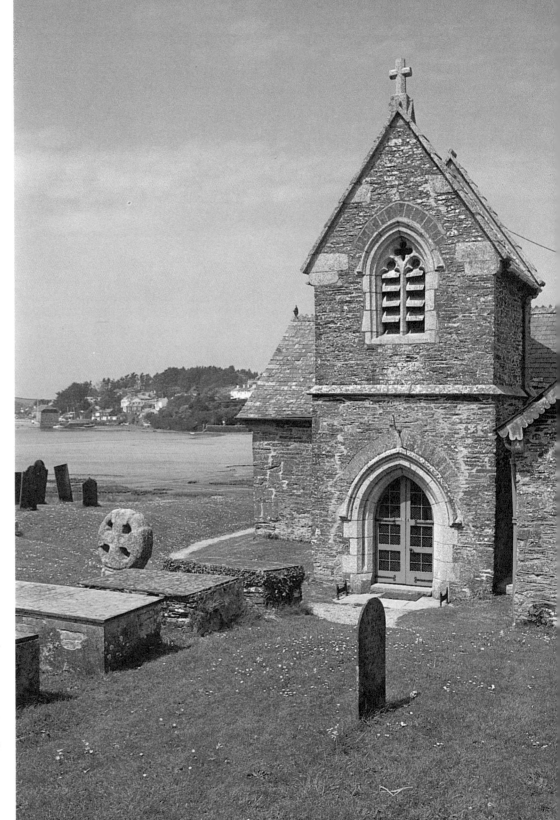

St Michael's, Porthilley, the churchyard golden with cowslips: '. . . its ancient setting still casts a spell.'

beginning to open for the summer season ahead and buckets and spades and sunshades and all the paraphernalia of beach holidays were being displayed outside the shops. It gave us a real holiday feeling and reminded me that the tourist trade is now one of Padstow's main sources of income.

Rock Quay through a window in St Michael's Church at Porthilly.

Once this harbour was a thriving port, offering shelter to ships which suffered the wild seas and treacherous cliffs of the north coast: a busy centre for the transport of copper, slate and stone, and famous for its ship building and fishing trade. Now there are all sorts of new plans for bringing the harbour back to life and making it more affluent and this is being done under the supervision of the harbour master who is Bill Lindsey's son.

As we boarded the ferry boat Bill introduced me to the ferryman, Peter McBurnie, whose father worked on the ferry with Bill for nine years. Many Padstow families are interlinked so that everyone seems related in some way or another through marriage, acquaintance or blood. Once you are accepted by Padstonians you have a marvellous feeling of protection.

Bill remembers with nostalgia the boats he owned when he ran the ferry crossing: *St Saviour's*, *St Minver*, *St Enodoc*, *St Petroc*. These early saints have all given their names to places in the area: St Petroc, who landed at the River Camel with sixty followers, to Padstow itself, for Petrocstowe was the old name for Padstow. Bill must have made the crossing between Rock and Padstow literally thousands of times: he has rowed it and sailed it and now enjoys the engine-driven journey.

His great grandfather was drowned on the Doom Bar, that dreaded sandbank where so many ships were sunk at the mouth of the estuary. He was going out to join an immigration ship when his boat overturned. It was a common occurrence, the Doom Bar being responsible for many terrible accidents in these waters.

The view as you look out to sea from the ferry crossing is dramatic and beautiful. There lie the two great headlands of Pentire and Stepper Point. There is an indentation in the last thrust of Stepper Point which Bill told me was blasted in the last war and the rubble used for the runway at St Merryn aerodrome.

I once walked out, on a windy winter day, to the

An aerial view of Rock with Harbour Cove and Stepper Point beyond. It is here at the mouth of the estuary that the Doom Bar lies.

Left: The spikes of the marsh orchid grow in damp, marshy hollows beside many Cornish rivers. Below: House martins newly arrived from Africa collect pellets of mud to build their domed nests under the eaves of buildings.

very end of Pentire Point. The gale was so powerful I felt I would be blown from that perch and I crouched low on the ground for safety, but it was thrilling to be there and to look down on the beaches and cliffs and rocks around. There is an atmosphere of danger and excitement that is always evident on the north coast of Cornwall.

I wondered what pictures from the past Bill conjured up as he looked out to sea from the ferry boat. He has worked hard all his life and considers himself a fortunate man, feeling he has given his best to the community. Recently he lost his wife, whom he married as a teenager, when she died after a long fight with cancer. Bill was desolate without the companion

St Minver Church – one of three beautiful churches in St Minver Parish.

of his life, but he set to work to raise money for the Mount Edgcumbe Hospice and raised over £6,000. Most of this was done by carving a long wooden chain and getting sponsorship for each well-worked link. He is indefatigably cheerful and one of the best companions with whom one could possibly hope to spend the day.

When I waved goodbye to Bill who was returning to Padstow, I walked across the sand below Rock to claim my car and go in search of the upper reaches of the Camel.

Rock and the adjoining golf course, owned by the Duchy of Cornwall, and the little church of St Enodoc, which has several times in history been buried by encroaching sands, are a world of their own.

This is always to me Betjeman land, for I learned about it and had the feel of the place through the Poet Laureate's poems and writings. He came there as a child on holiday and later wrote about the sand dunes and the golf course and St Enodoc Church. It was most poignant that while I was writing this chapter Sir John Betjeman's death was announced. He lies at St Enodoc, where his mother was buried before him. Come on!

> Come on! Come on! This hillock hides the spire,
> Now that one and now none. As winds about
> The burnished path through lady's finger, thyme,
> And bright varieties of saxifrage,
> So grows the tinny tenor faint or loud
> And all things draw towards St Enodoc.

Thus he wrote when remembering his early years of worship at the church.

In the early 1800s the church was buried by the shifting sands and I like to think of the vicar who had to enter the church through a skylight in the roof in order to keep the tithes.

During the winter months, in recent years, I came

> *'So grows the tinny tenor faint or loud*
> *And all things draw towards St Enodoc.'*
> *Sir John Betjeman.*

to Rock with family and friends and spent three days walking in the wild winds and rain when there were few people about. There is something most exhilarating about the sands and cliffs of this part of Cornwall when the elements are at their harshest.

There are three very beautiful churches in the parish of St Minver: St Enodoc, St Minver and the little church of St Michael at Porthilly. To reach the church of St Michael we walked through the adjoining farmyard; the farm is thought to have been an ecclesiastical building attached to the church at one time. The church has been largely restored over the years but its ancient setting still casts a spell. It is situated right by the water and though this part of the estuary has largely silted up there is evidence that once people came to church by water: little stone steps lead up from the river bed to the church door.

The churchyard was full of wild cowslips when I went there in early May. I had never seen so many growing in one place for many years. There is also a fine granite cross outside the church door which is a rare holed cross dating from the fifth to the eighth century. The original purpose of such a cross was to mark a holy place or preaching station. There is a strong possibility that this church was on the old Pilgrims' Way from Ireland via Cornwall to Rome. Many saints and missionaries travelled across Cornwall, landing at Padstow and making their way overland to the Fowey estuary, thus avoiding the hazardous route around Land's End.

An earlier crossing on the Rock ferry with Cassock Hill in the background. 'St Christopher takes many forms . . .'

Modern stories of Rock still find men coming by water and falling in love with the surrounding countryside and staying on.

One such man is Ken Duxbury who has been a sailor and writer all his life. He first sailed into the Camel estuary in his forty-foot Whitstable oyster boat *Thyra* in 1955. He liked the estuary and the surrounding coastline so much that he made Rock his base, sold his boat at the end of 1956 and started giving sailing lessons off Ferry Point, Rock in 1957. Three years later, together with Ken Robertson and Trevor Evans, he formed a team which became the highly successful Westerly School of Sailing and the boatbuilding firm of Westerly Boats (Dinghy Specialists Ltd). In 1970 Ken sold his shares in the business to take up writing full time and now lives on Bodmin Moor from where he says, 'On a clear day I can see whether the tide is in or out at Old Town Cove and Cant Creek.'

I think Ken Duxbury's poem, which he wrote while waiting for the ferry at Ferry Point one rain-washed day, is most evocative of this part of the river's life.

On sodden slope of shining sand, forsaken by the tide
The Moment's brief recording hand disconsolately scribes
My footprints' thin, erratic, line,
Soppy sockets filled with brine
From marram grass to waterline
— custom for the ferry.

Oozy soplets, icy droplets
Grey rain splashing down in ploplets
Surely now he'll see me standing
Hopefully at the Ferry landing?

Padstow: you can almost wade it — so near and yet so far,
Three minutes in the Ferryboat, and sixteen miles by car!
But this is Cornwall — give him time,
Unpunctuality's no crime
… Alfie's just not ready.

Shimmer, shiver, wind-whipped river.
Effortlessly flow and sever
All connection, like a moat.
Blast that tardy Ferryboat!

As thunder-surf of Doom has broken pulses from a deeper ocean
So the gull's discordant scream breaks the rhythm of a dream.
I hunch my back against the wind and hope the rain won't trickle in
And watch the August Heavens spill black torrents over Cassock Hill.
I'll murder Alfie… so I will!

Ah! Echo-edge of engine throbbing?
The mirage-twisted boat comes bobbing,
Weaving Rockwards through the storm
— St Christopher takes many forms!

So, sallow, swart and leather tanned,
Wrecker-spawned, he comes to land…
I walk the ribbed plank, grasp the hand,
Smile…
And PAY the ferryman.

If you don't use the pedestrian ferry at Rock, then the next crossing by car is the bridge at Wadebridge, four miles up the estuary.

Left: Mrs Winifred Beare at Hingham Mill with her great grandson and great niece.
Right: The late Arnold Beare ground the wheat for family and friends.

The estuary of the River Camel is considered to be one of the best bird sanctuaries in Cornwall and now that the railway has been closed there is a fine footpath from Wadebridge to Padstow which is one of the best places to see a great variety of river bird life. An osprey is seen in the area most years, also the peregrine falcon and sandpipers. Shellduck, the attractive clearly marked black and white birds with red beaks, nest nearby in rabbit holes to protect their eggs from seagulls.

The Cornwall Trust for Nature Conservation has done much work to protect areas such as the Camel Estuary and, unlike many other conservation organisations, they have worked in close harmony with farmers and local inhabitants to retain all that is best in wildlife and plants.

As you leave behind the tidal reaches of the estuary and the town of Wadebridge, which was once navigable by large vessels and where boatbuilding used to be a major activity, the Camel flows through very different scenery. It makes its way past wooded slopes, little villages, farmland, and then runs below some of the wildest parts of Bodmin Moor so that often looking up from a wooded valley with an old stone bridge you will see a dramatic background of tors and rocks and barren hilltops.

The River Camel is often referred to as the 'river which changed its mind', or the 'crooked river'. It wends its way southward and then suddenly changes its direction above Bodmin and turns northward, so that it begins and ends its life on the north side of Cornwall.

While following the river upstream I found many peaceful crossing places where ancient stone bridges and wooded slopes make for unique settings. Near Sladesbridge the River Camel is joined by one of its main tributaries, the Allen River, and not far from the meeting place of these two rivers we found an old mill house called Hingham where the water wheel still does its work and grinds corn for the farmer's family and friends.

Winifred Beare lives there and she showed us around. Sadly her husband Arnold died recently and so she is not sure who will keep the mill running now. Mrs Beare remembers the mill working for many years for her father-in-law ran it before her husband. She told me that there used to be seven or eight mills working on the Allen River, but most of them have been converted to electric methods.

Further up river just below the moorland town of Blisland at Merry Meeting we were to find another working mill which I believe is the only water wheel still doing commercial work in Cornwall.

Mr and Mrs Rodney Keat were able to show us

around their mill. Here they crush hundreds of tons of grain every year. I loved the heavy thumping sound of the water wheel turning the crusher, like a steady heart beat with enormous power, all coming from a little stream which feeds the River Camel. The Keat family are well-known millers. They have been involved in milling for at least three generations.

Lavethan Mills, Merry Meeting. 'I believe it is the only water wheel still doing commercial work in Cornwall.'

Seeing how these streams can generate such power is impressive and made me wonder if one day we could not turn the clocks back and revitalize the many old water mills that exist in the area. The method is simple and yet most effective without marring the peaceful countryside.

Gam Bridge, Helland Bridge, Wenford Bridge are all crossing places on the River Camel of exceptional beauty. Wenford Bridge became famous for the pottery started near there by Michael Cardew who became one of the best known and most respected of Cornish potters. Now, just above Helland Bridge there is another potter called Paul Jackson, who has named his pottery after the bridge. He does some unusual work which is most attractive using gentle colours— blues, yellows, greens—and wonderful designs of humming birds, fishes and flowers. His shapes are generous and rounded and he likes to work on larger bowls, pots and urns as well as the smaller items. Although his work is beautiful enough to stand on its decorative merit it is also practical and much of his pottery is oven proof.

Sitting below his workshop on Helland Bridge I watched the river flowing past the grey stone houses, one covered in a beautiful flowering wisteria. An old gentleman was walking slowly towards me in the sunshine. We stood together looking around us in silence for a while. Then he said slowly, 'Perfect spot isn't it?' I smiled in agreement and he told me that he came often to enjoy the gentle scenery and the peace of the place.

Just above the bridge the old railway once ran and when you cross the line on the lane leading up to the moor you can see an old signal box which has been transformed into a quaint little house.

Not far from Helland Bridge lies the great house of Pencarrow. Home of the Molesworth family it is open to the public during the summer months. Grand and grey it stands amongst wooded land of great beauty and in the early spring when I drove along that part of

Right: The bridge at Wadebridge, originally 320 feet long and a mere nine feet wide with seventeen Gothic arches.

The Author talks to Mr and Mrs Keat at Lavethan Mills.

the valley the bright sunlight filtered through the translucent green of the trees, just coming into leaf. Every view, every slope and winding lane was brightened by the new growth in hedgerows brilliant with campion and bluebells.

After I had spent four days wandering along the River Camel from its mouth at Padstow and Rock, along the estuary to the grand old bridge at Wadebridge, which can boast to have been there for five

hundred years and was, according to Carew in his Elizabethan *Survey*, 'the longest, the strongest and the fairest that the shire can muster', then to the narrower reaches upstream, over little stone bridges and through wooded valleys below the gaunt moorland, I was reminded again and again of the mingling of the best of old and new which exists in Cornwall.

It may be peaceful now but years ago, all along the Camel, Iron Age hill forts were built to control the inhabitants or quell marauders. There is an excavated Roman fort at Nanstallon on the River Camel just west of Bodmin which provides a picture of a Roman

Pencarrow House, home of the
Molesworth family.

Sir John Molesworth St Aubyn
talking to Sir John Tremayne.

*Helland Bridge: 'He told me he came often to
enjoy the gentle scenery and the peace . . .'*

garrison at work. This fort was occupied until AD
75-80.

No one can spend time on the Camel River without
being aware of the spirit of King Arthur. The legends
are linked to many of the towns, villages and hill forts
in the area.

Was Camelford his Camelot? Did King Arthur
fight his last battle high up on the early reaches of the
river?

Is Slaughterbridge—that beautiful old bridge with
its rough-hewn stone supports—where Arthur died?
Is the vast granite block called Arthur's Grave which
lies nearby really his burial stone? Or is it the head-
stone of some other gallant Celtic chief?

I have come to realize that facts are unimportant
where the legends of King Arthur are concerned. It is
the Spirit of chivalry, of good conquering evil, of
valour and of good comradeship which lingers on.
Where Arthur led we still believe we can follow.

And nowhere has the spirit of Arthur been so
revitalised over the years as in Cornwall. People, who

*The Author talking to Paul Jackson who has
named his pottery after the bridge. He uses gentle
colours for his designs of humming birds, fishes
and flowers.*

made their living in a tough and strenuous manner, in fishing, mining or on the land, used these legends to colour their lives and they do not intend to let them die out now, or let them be claimed by another county.

Now there are fishermen, farmers, potters, miners, boatbuilders and those who cater for the tourist trade who live along the Camel, but those who went before have left their mark—layers of history and legend are spread across the countryside.

Gam Bridge crosses the River Camel below St Breward on the edge of Bodmin Moor. The valley is very steep here.

The River Fowey

The Fowey River, which links the moorland of Cornwall with the great port and fishing town of Fowey, seems to me to have three different parts to its story.

Beginning up on the wildest part of Bodmin Moor it has a stark and legend-filled side to its character. Later it wends its way below great houses and castles and here is its grandest facet. At its end it opens up to the sea in a fine estuary banked on one side by Fowey town and on the other by the villages of Polruan and Bodinnick.

To see Fowey town at its best it is exciting to cross on the ancient ferry from Bodinnick. From there you can see the town spreading down the steep sides with some houses built right out over the harbour.

No wonder this was once the most loved of towns for such a man of letters as Sir Arthur Quiller Couch. He wrote about it, lived in it and treasured his relationship with the town and its people above all else.

His daughter, Foy, he named after the river and she became a friend of Dame Daphne du Maurier when the authoress first came as a young girl to live at Bodinnick and wrote her first book *The Loving Spirit*. The house at Bodinnick is still owned by her sister

Angela du Maurier (left) still lives at Ferryside (right) at Bodinnick, where Daphne du Maurier wrote her first novel as a girl.

Angela and was once the habitat of boatbuilders and sailmakers.

On the house you can see the figurehead from an old sailing vessel, rescued by Daphne du Maurier and friends, and around which she based the story of her first novel. In the little creeks, coves and 'pills', as they are called here, around Fowey harbour, there are all sorts of hidden beauty spots. Intermingling with it all huge ships wend their way continuously up river to be loaded with their cargo of china clay. Perhaps it is the variety of scenery and activity that gives Fowey its very special character, perhaps it is its history of smuggling and fearless seamen who stood out against the French who came to plunder the town. Perhaps it is the blockhouses which stand on each side of the harbour from where a great iron chain was once slung to keep out unwelcome visitors.

Some even say that Jesus, as a boy, came with Joseph of Arimathea and landed on the rocks below Polruan. A white cross is erected there at the point called Punche's Cross—the story of Christ's boyhood visit to Britain has persisted down the ages and is perpetuated in the singing of William Blake's fine hymn:

And did those feet in ancient time
Walk upon England's mountains green
And was the Holy Lamb of God
On England's pleasant pastures seen?

On the hill above the cross are the remains of an old chapel called St Saviour's. There was another chapel on the Camel Estuary also called St Saviours and both these buildings were guides to the sailors who came on the pilgrim route through Cornwall from the Continent to Ireland or vise versa. The first records of the chapel at Polruan date from 1284 but a chapel existed there some hundreds of years earlier, probably from the eighth or ninth centuries.

Fowey is as famous for its launching and welcoming

Looking across to Polruan from Fowey.

of pilgrims as it is for its later more lurid history of marauders and 'gallants', smugglers and privateers.

When the Celtic Church was at its most powerful, and later in the fifteenth century when the pilgrims went to Spain to visit the shrine of St James at Compostella, they also journeyed to the shrine at St Michael's Mount. They often arrived along the coast from Plymouth and then travelled overland to the Fal

The view from Hall Walk opposite Fowey.

crossing by King Harry Ferry and then on to St Day and the Mount.

This great movement of religious leaders and their followers was evident through hundreds of years of Cornish history and has inevitably left a connection of religious centres throughout the county, particularly by rivers and their havens and estuaries. The link between Cornwall and Brittany was founded on the Celtic religion, flourished through the later trading between the countries and to this day holds fast.

I once went in search of the source of the Fowey River. It was a bitter winter that year, but not wanting to wait until the milder spring climate came, and with a kind of fascination for this rough and barren land of Bodmin Moor in winter months, I set out when the snow still lay in great drifts round the river banks.

It was a hard walk, and the mists nearly enclosed us before we managed to find our way back to civilisation but nonetheless it proved worthwhile.

There was something uniquely exciting about finding the first gushing rivulets of the river which I knew led to so many different places on its long journey down to Fowey town.

There, in the gathering dusk, I stood with my two companions, looking out across the moor, trying to discern those famous peaks Brown Willy and Roughtor, and feeling cut off from the rest of the world, more in touch with the Bronze Age men who once lived and worked here.

We had trudged through boggy land, lost our gum boots and pulled them from the mud, but keeping always close to the little river, knowing through it we found some sort of security. There was something particularly wonderful in realizing and witnessing that a river is re-born every second of its life. Forever more new waters must flow from here down to the sea. At one time the moorland was called Fowey Moor after the river.

Bodmin Moor not only gives life to rivers; I never go there myself but I feel a new sense of energy. It is not a place that everyone will love. Its gauntness and loneliness can reject many people, and yet be the very breath of life to others.

The farmers who farm just below Bolventor are people who respect the land; some of them would never live anywhere else but they do not sentimentalise the place. They talk of its hardships, and its drawbacks, and the terrible winters they have known, with a kind of admiration.

I think one of the most remarkable characters I ever met was Joe Halls. He had lived and farmed on the moor all his life and always swore he could not live

The Author with Joe Halls, his wife and family at Carkeet on Bodmin Moor.

58

Brown Willy, the highest point in Cornwall. 'The Moor not only gives life to rivers . . . it can be the very breath of life to some people.'

anywhere else. I realised how much change a man like Joe Halls had seen in the last fifty years of farming when he told me that he had never had electric light and thought the motorcar had done more to 'ruin the quality of life' than anything else he had known.

He had walked, as a younger man, to chapel at least once a Sunday. At that time St Luke's Chapel at Bolventor had been the meeting place for all chapel people in the area and farmers would walk from miles away, carrying lanterns in their hands, like glow-worms, their gentle lights eventually homing in on the chapel.

Cattle were then rounded up on horseback, fires were fed with peat dug from the moors, and the houses and field walls were constructed from the moorland granite.

A group of farmers from this area once drove me, again in the winter, on to the top of the moor overlooking the Fowey valley to see a piece of commonland called Draynes Common. Its 196 acres are totally enclosed by a great granite stone wall that must have been built over a hundred years ago and still stands well enough to fence in their cattle.

There they showed me the old remnants of two stone cutters' cottages. Those men had lived there in the early part of this century, cutting the granite for pig troughs, gate posts and other necessary implements of a farmer's life. Somehow the old fruit trees and bushes, now tumbled and rotten, that they had planted to make some sort of garden around their meagre dwellings, seemed sad reminders of a time past. The stone cutters were apparently paid five gold sovereigns by the Coryton family of the Pentillie

Golitha Falls: '. . . the light filters through the trees and the sound of water is ever present.'

Left: The village of Golant perched on the water's edge.

Above and left: St Winnow Church. 'The light glances off grey tombstones and the square granite tower.'

Estate, who once owned Draynes Common, to remove themselves from the land when it was sold.

There is so much history interwoven with the moor like this. There in the middle of nowhere amongst the heather and the bracken, lie ancient milestones ... '7 miles to Liskeard' one reads. From traces of old tracks we know that across this part of the moor men drove their cattle, even from as far away as Somerset— coming to sell and to buy at Liskeard.

Standing up on Draynes Common that day I looked around me at all the tors and slanting horizons, bare and untouched by man. I remarked to one of the farmers, 'Isn't it beautiful?' ... He turned away, glancing at the mists rolling in from the coast. 'It's all right in the summer,' he said. Like a man who no longer tells his wife how beautiful she is, these farmers do not see or remark on their surroundings, but have learned how to live with the moor and could not live without it.

'It is exciting to cross on the ferry at Bodinnick.'

Below Draynes Common, past Trekievesteps, where once a thriving village school was in action, Draynes Bridge crosses the River Fowey. With that natural sense of history that the Cornish have I was once told the story of how the last King of Cornwall, King Doniert, was drowned when his horse fell here in a swollen, flooding river. Just above the river you can still see King Doniert's burial stone. It reads *Doniert rogavet pro anima* — 'Doniert asks prayers for his soul'.

Leading down from Draynes bridge to the Golitha waterfalls which tumble down in a spectacular way over huge worn boulders, is a magnificent avenue of beech trees with their great and tangled roots reaching out towards the river. It is one of the loveliest walks in summer when the light is filtered through the trees and the sound of the water is ever present. In the

spring wild flowers in the nearby woods are a sight many local people come to see and it is a much loved picnic spot although never overpopulated.

So the early part of the Fowey's character is built around the harsh beauty of the moor and the early ramblings across boulders, under little ancient bridges and through wooded avenues, but soon it opens out into a wider water-meadowed countryside, passing through farmland and the Glyn Valley. The great house of the area, Glynn House, was once occupied by the family of the same name but fell into a state of disrepair. Now it has been totally restored by a Doctor Peter Mitchell who was awarded the Nobel Prize for chemistry in 1978 and who has done a fine job on the house and grounds.

On the other side of the river, not far from the rail road, is another great and beautiful house, Lanhydrock. This house is now owned by the National Trust but was once the home of the Liberal family, the Robartes.

Although the house was almost entirely destroyed by fire in 1881 it has been so beautifully restored that the character and atmosphere is very much that of a much older house.

The Robartes family were Roundheads and were in danger when the King's men captured Respryn Bridge, at the end of Lanhydrock drive, and tried to force Robartes and his companions out. Sir Richard Grenville did capture the house for a time, and Lord Robartes and his friends were forced to make their escape by sea to Plymouth. When Cromwell finally won his victory Lord Robartes planted a famous sycamore avenue to mark the occasion.

It is a great house, and the approach through the marvellous parkland is most impressive. Loveliest of all the rooms is the Gallery, 116 feet long and with a fine moulded ceiling. This room was the only one which was almost untouched in the fire. It is still used for concerts and the Duchy Ball which takes place at Lanhydrock each year at Christmas time.

This part of the river's life has its grandest connections. Not far from Lanhydrock the river wends its way past one of the finest castles in Cornwall, and Cornwall has more than its fair share of these grand fortified remains.

Some sort of fortification has existed at Restormel since 1100. The great heiress Isolda de Cardinham owned the castle in the early thirteenth century but she bequeathed it to her overlord Richard, Earl of Cornwall in 1270. In 1229 the Earldom of Cornwall reverted to the Crown and since that day Restormel has belonged to the Earldom—later the Duchy—of Cornwall which forms an apanage of the King's or Queen's eldest son. The Black Prince, the first Duke of Cornwall, lived at the castle in the fourteenth century and it was used as a stronghold in the seventeenth century during the Civil War.

Pont: 'The Fowey River is interspersed with creeks of great beauty and atmosphere.'

The history of the place is fascinating and closely linked with the town of Lostwithiel below, where Earl Edmund of Cornwall built the famous Duchy Palace, then the Royal Palace. At that time Lostwithiel was a stannary town where the tinners brought their blocks of metal to be weighed, assayed and stamped. The river has now silted up to a great extent and no longer can one see the great sailing vessels that came with their cargoes as far as the bridge at Lostwithiel.

However, the history and the ancient grandeur remain to make it a town with a strong community feeling and intermingling of the best of the old and the new. The main road skirts the prettiest part of the town and it is possible to pass through Lostwithiel without ever looking up to see Restormel on the one hand, or wandering down to the river and savouring the real feeling of the town.

The church spire is long and slender, and unusual for Cornwall. It is a great landmark in the area, but you come upon it with surprise, nestled between the shops.

John Betjeman wrote: 'Lostwithiel has more to show in a small space than any Cornish town', and this is surely true.

Each day the trains come and go from the station at Lostwithiel carrying trucks of china clay down to Fowey where the cargo is loaded onto the great vessels that take the valuable produce all over the

world. I once travelled on a china clay train and marvelled at the beautiful scenery, passing the village of Golant, perched on the water's edge. The railway runs right by the river and the view across to the other side, to gentle hills and wooded banks, with every kind of river bird to be seen, is quite staggering.

Above the village of Golant lies the squat, stoic little church dedicated to St Sampson, one of Cornwall's more famous Celtic saints who came to convert and did so with great success, travelling on to Brittany. At the church there are links with the great legend of Tristan and Iseult. Tradition has it that King Mark brought his bride Iseult here and she bequeathed her wedding dress to the church as a memento.

Nearby is another holy place with equal charm but a place so peaceful it would be hard to find its equal.

It is one of the places I beg people visiting Cornwall to go and see, for it is unique, I believe, in its quality of light and in its secluded beauty. Water always adds a new dimension to views and landscapes, and maybe this is why I have learned to love so many riverside places, but St Winnow Church, perched right by the water, with its small hamlet of houses, remains for me

one of the most perfect places in Cornwall. The light glances off grey tombstones, the granite square tower of the church and rich fields and woods around. Inside, the church has some rare fifteenth-century stained-glass windows with rich deep blues, greens and reds. One marvels that such works of art have lasted through so many restorations and dilapidations. There are also some old carved bench-ends as primitively beautiful as the glass windows. Inside and out St Winnow Church is full of a rich pure beauty that is as much felt as seen.

The Fowey River is interspersed with creeks of great beauty and atmosphere. Further down river, below Golant, is the Old Sawmills Creek which has the same quiet, secluded, magical feeling and Penpoll Creek is also endowed with another Celtic hermitage, now a house belonging to the author and historian Raleigh Trevelyan.

Hills, slanting fields, many of which retain ancient names, thick woods, and the added attraction of water that comes and goes with the tides, all add together to make the beauty of these places. You can return in different weathers, on bright frosty days, in the rain that is so familiar in Cornwall, or on warm mellow autumn days when the trees are changing their colours. Each time the light is different, there is something new to see and comprehend, but the essence of tranquillity is always there.

These are the last silent, peaceful parts of the river before it enters the bustling town of Fowey itself and on to the sea.

Life may have changed tremendously over the last four hundred years in Fowey. Certainly there is no longer the fear of invasion as there so often was. The Dutch and the French do not threaten, the smugglers no longer stop and plunder ships that put to sea, and the blockhouses, which lie either side of the harbour are places of beauty to admire but no longer used as defensive buildings.

But Fowey has remained a busy place. Because of

Fowey harbour has remained a busy place. Great cargo ships come from all over the world to load china clay.

In hot weather, butterflies such as the painted lady come down to drink at the edges of streams and rivers.

The pied wagtail bears the nickname of 'dishwasher' in the Westcountry.

The great house of Place can be seen with its tall conspicuous tower looking down on the river.

the china clay being loaded here, the river traffic has not died out. It has changed dramatically in shape and size: looking back to some of the earliest photographs of Fowey Town we can see that all the ships were still under sail. Now they come from all over the world, great cargo ships, carefully wending their way between the smaller vessels that litter the harbour, intent on their work and their trade.

The great house of Place, the home for hundreds of years of the famous Treffry family, can be seen with its tall conspicuous tower looking down on the river. It is unusual to see the mansion of the town built so closely amongst the shops and cottages and other buildings. Perhaps for this reason it has become closely associated with the history of Fowey.

During the French invasion in 1457 when the town was burned and plundered, Elizabeth Treffry, in the absence of her husband, defended the house by instructing her staff to pour melted lead on the enemy below. The house to this day seems like a fort against all dangers. Leland, who stayed at Place in 1538, said: 'Thomas Treffry builded a right fair and strong embatelid Tour in his House; and embateling al the walles of the House in a manner made it a Castelle.'

Below Place is the historic church of St Fimbarrus.

Below the house is the historic church of St Fimbarrus. Its majestic proportions are missed unless one walks around it and into it. It is dedicated to an Irish Saint Finn Barr who became the first Bishop of Cork and died there in 604. He made a pilgrimage to Rome and it is believed he could have travelled by Fowey on that occasion. Many of the saints at that time travelled across the land from Padstow estuary to that of Fowey when on their journeys.

John Keast, the Cornish historian who wrote a history of Fowey town, ended his book with this paragraph: 'Yet still the life of the old town goes on. Still men scheme and plan, young folk marry and have children to gladden their lives and in time see their grandchildren about them. The rhythm of life continues—rising and falling, but rising again—as the tides that lap the quay side. It is the rhythm of the million tides which have ebbed and flowed since St Finn Barr left his name in this part of Cornwall. And mingling unseen with the tides is the constant, unfailing, flow of the river, coming down from the quiet moors — the divine purpose, as it were, running through the ebb and flow of human endeavour.'

The narrow streets of Fowey Town.

The River Lynher

The Tamar is a grand river, the Falmouth peaceful, the Helford hidden, the Fowey romantic, the Camel wild and northerly and more rugged in its beauty, but the brightest and best for me will always be the Lynher.

I cannot be impartial, brought up as I was on the banks of the Lynher at my grandfather's house, Pencrebar, just outside Callington.

Later I spent endless happy holidays with my parents in the Duchy of Cornwall's Castle, Trematon, where they made their home for twenty years. Now, in the last six months, my family and I have made our home by the Lynher where the river views are seen from every window.

It is not only familiarity which makes it my favourite of all rivers, it is also the great variety of scenery through which it flows: from early moorland to the last grand reaches where it passes manor houses and castles, eventually joining the Tamar at the Hamoaze with its naval moorings.

I have always known about the wooded slopes that meet the moor below Hawks Tor and which form the ancient estate of Trebartha but had never visited it until I was researching this book. Then I was lucky enough to be invited for a beautiful walk through the woods and grounds of Trebartha by Rosemary Latham, just one of the members of the Latham family who own the 3,000 acres of land surrounding the early life of the Lynher.

The estate was owned for over 200 years by the

'I was lucky enough to be invited for a beautiful walk through the woods and grounds of Trebartha by Rosemary Latham . . .'

Two views of the Withy Brook at Trebartha.

Port Eliot at St Germans: 'Once the water came right up to the house . . .'

'The present Lord Eliot has recently added a maze to the grounds . . .'

Rodd family who were well known as popular land-owners and members of the community and it was not until 1940 that they sold it to the Latham family. It is such a grand place, so unusual, with its terraces and lake and American gardens and the marvellous waterfalls formed by Withy Brook which joins the Lynher on the estate. It is the contrast of moor and thick woods and water which is so exciting. I don't think that in all my life I have so enjoyed a part of the country which I had long imagined in my mind's eye and which lived on through stories I was told or read.

When Mr Bryan Latham bought the estate from the Rodd family it was the first time that it had changed hands through a sale. Previous to that it had either been inherited through family connections or by ancient decrees.

Bryan Latham, who died recently, wrote a history and evocative description of the estate called *Trebartha, The House by the Stream*, this being the literal translation of the Cornish name.

In it he describes going to view the estate, being taken for a walk by the keeper, falling in love with the woods and grounds, taking his wife and children to see it so that they too fell under its spell, and then persuading his father that it was a sensible and reasonable transaction to buy it.

The old manor house was pulled down in 1948 and I went to stand on the foundations to get a sense of the view and surroundings Trebartha Hall once enjoyed. The stables and walled garden, which still exist, lie close to the setting of the house and once almost adjoined the building with a courtyard between, so that all the activities of stable, garden and household must have been closely linked.

The real glory of the place is in the amalgamation of the trees, the water, the craggy outline of Hawks Tor which overlooks the whole estate from a thousand feet above, and the fact that the River Lynher makes its way through the fields and woods and hills that surround it.

Withy Brook which falls over great boulders down through the woods from the moor above is one of the most beautiful sights and its waterfalls have long been named The Cascades. I talked to Olive Lawry who used to live at nearby Lynher Farm with her family and she remembers walking there when she was a child and knowing the landscape intimately. Once in a fearfully cold winter the Cascades froze into picturesque great icicles which transformed the whole scenery.

The property is private but the Latham family open the grounds to the public two or three times a year for charity and it is well worth taking the opportunity to visit Trebartha for it is unique and quite spell-binding.

My connections with the Lynher River go back before my birth, for when my father was a schoolboy and living in Plymouth with his family he used to go to Lynher Farm for holidays to stay with the Lawrys who were old family friends.

I have listened to him, over the years, telling stories of how they rode the cart horses to Coads Green to have them shod and the fun they had enjoying the busy life on the farm. These remain some of his happiest childhood memories and when I visited the farm, still owned by the Lawry family, I could see what a wonderful place it was for childhood pastimes. Sadly the farmhouse was badly damaged by fire last year but it is being carefully restored.

'Once in a fearfully cold winter the Cascades at Trebartha froze into great icicles . . .'

My father used to go to Lynher Farm for holidays as a boy.

North Hill has an unexpectedly impressive church.

Between Lynher Farm and Trebartha Estate is the little village of North Hill with its unexpectedly impressive church. It never fails to thrill me when arriving in the village to see the staunch and important tower of North Hill rising above the slate-roofed buildings. The bossed barrel roof of the church, the carvings and monuments to the Rodds and the Spoures, their predecessors at Trebartha, all make it a dignified and surprisingly grand church for such a humble, and yet beautifully unspoilt, moor-side setting.

From North Hill down river the countryside becomes more gentle and full of secret nooks and crannies that are rarely visited by the outside world.

A friend recently showed me a beautiful little manor house dating from 1653. The original part of the building is medieval, the newest addition and much of the interior still intact with a rare barrel vaulted ceiling, ornate mouldings and ancient oak carved doors and granite mullion windows. I don't think I have ever been to a house which is so little known and so little changed. Down below in a deep cut valley lies the River Lynher and from the house you can hear the rush of a little stream which joins the river below. Although its state of preservation must be almost unique in the area, its atmosphere, the silence and seclusion are typical of this part of the River Lynher between Bathpool and Rilla Mill.

Rilla Mill is a very pretty riverside village with the old mill house, a fine bridge and a wide water meadow. There are some wonderful Cornish names of houses, farms and hamlets in the area; Trewoodloe, Tregonnett, Trevigro and others.

Michael Horrell and his family have farmed Duchy land near Rilla Mill for three generations. Michael is responsible for farming 500 acres of land in this area and has become a famous farmer with his Methodist connections and his part-time journalism.

Recently his farm has become the home of a local cheese which is made at the Lynher Valley Dairies. The cheese was the idea of Allen and Jenny Gray, who produced the recipe, but it was Michael who gave the cheese a home and has done much to help its marketing in the area. Called Yarg—the name Gray spelt backwards—it is made from the milk produced

Mrs Rodd, the Squire's wife (in the striped dress),
attends a Red Cross sewing meeting during the
First World War.

NORTH HILL

WORKING PARTY

The Lynher below Cadsonbury
– playground of my youth.

'The house of my childhood, Pencrebar, stands above the river.'

on the farm and is matured in nettle leaves which Margaret Horrell told me are picked by children from the area and kept in the deep freeze until needed.

The cheese was first put on the market just before Christmas 1983 and since then has proved very popular, selling well in Cornwall where people are often dubious of new ideas.

However, the bridge and hamlet I know and love best is Newbridge on the outskirts of Callington, and all along the river from here to Clapper Bridge I count as the playground of my youth.

The house of my childhood, Pencrebar, stands above the river. We used to walk down through the woods from there, or ride our ponies, and play endless games on the wooded banks. We sailed our paper boats, paddled in the water, climbed from one little island to the next playing imagined games of hide and seek, often falling into the river and returning home wet and bedraggled to be scolded by our elders and betters—but never by our grandfather who remained implacably indulgent.

We rode down, when the holidays came, to have our ponies shod at the smithy by the water, which sadly no longer exists, and I can remember so clearly the burning smell of hot horse hoof as the iron shoes

were welded to their shape. I loved the day's outing, the sound of iron being beaten, the bellows making the burning embers flare, and the deft expertise and precision of the blacksmith's work.

Sometimes our grandfather would set a race and name a prize to the top of Cadsonbury, the old Iron Age fort which rises above the river. We would scramble up, cutting our knees on brambles, forcing our way through bracken, gasping for breath on the steep man-made slope at the top. I never won, there was always a cousin or a brother faster than me, but who cared, there was always a consolation prize.

We were brought up on a heady dose of enthusiasm, by our grandfather and aunts and uncles, for the place in which we lived and its surroundings and that expansive love for the area has lasted all through my life.

When I walk now, below Newbridge, along the river, the memories of happy uncomplicated childhood days come flooding back in great waves of nostalgia.

Further down river lies Clapper Bridge whose surroundings are so pretty that local people have always ventured there for a quiet break and to enjoy the scenery. The water, bright and clear, rushes under

77

The view from my garden today.

the bridge and for many years we have used it as a family picnicking place so that my children remember it as a part of their childhood as it was of mine. The wooded slopes and farm fields are all enclosing and give it a protected air. When I went there this spring, sheep with their new born lambs grazed in an adjoining field in bright sunshine. I remembered the frantic childhood excitement that would transmit from one to another as we played enthusiastic games of Pooh Sticks. Dropping our sticks one side of the bridge, rushing down river to see whose stick came through first, yelling and screaming as if we were encouraging horses in a race. How simple the pleasures we enjoyed, how excited we all became.

There must be many people visiting Cornwall who drive along the main road from Saltash to Liskeard and see the sign that indicates Notter Bridge; perhaps this is the only time they are aware they are near to the River Lynher. There is a popular pub here where people come in the summer months to sit and enjoy the river, but it is far more populated than the quieter stretches between Newbridge and Clapper Bridge.

The River Lynher is still referred to as the Lynher or St German's River and below Notter Bridge it is joined by the Tiddy which flows past the village of St Germans with its ancient church and house, Port Eliot.

Once the water came right up to the house of Port Eliot, but it was drained away by the first Lord Eliot who inherited the house in 1748 from his father who had done a great deal in extending and adorning the building. The complicated system of underwater drains, sluices and culverts, which drained away the tidal water from a stream flowing into the River Tiddy, is still in use today.

The water approach had at one time been a great attribute of the house, church and monastery which once existed there, for until the late eighteenth century water travel by river or sea was easily the safest and easiest form of travel. It was not until the eighteenth century that the house was completely cut off from direct water access.

The first written record of the church at St Germans is in 936 when King Athelstan arrived by river in order to set up a bishopric. In 1185 these canons were suppressed and it became an Augustinian Priory. The monks remained until its dissolution in 1539.

The house and church lie side by side and are impressive in their simple beauty. The parkland and grounds roll away from the house in gentle hills. The whole situation has come a long way since Tonkin described it as 'facing north on the River Lynher which opens into a large basin before the house, very pleasant when the tide is in but something offensive when it is out from the smell of ouse and mud'.

The present Lord Eliot has recently added a maze to the grounds which he hopes will be fully grown within the next five to seven years. He has done much to popularise the estate by holding a vast folk festival there each year called The Elephant Fayre. Musicians and actors and craftsmen come from all over the country to take part in the fair and thousands of people congregate to sample the many types of entertainment.

The church, house, and surrounding village still feel very much part of a community. John Betjeman described St Germans as 'A Kingdom of its own'.

The Quay at St Germans was once extremely busy

St Erney Church above the Lynher.

with trading vessels and the ferrying of stone from many of the surrounding quarries, but much of the trade died away when the railway came. The viaduct which carried the trains runs over the quayside and is a marvellous sight.

Below St Germans the River Tiddy joins the Lynher and widens to give magnificent views to the houses thereabouts including Grove House belonging to Mr and Mrs J. Foster. From here the extensive panorama includes the Lynher and Erth Barton with its adjoining chapel and farmland belonging to Mr Richard Carew Pole, who now lives with his wife and two sons at the family house of Antony. Ten years ago he and his

wife Mary restored the house of Erth Barton and brought it back to life.

On these last wide reaches of the Lynher River lie some of the loveliest houses of Cornwall. Ince Castle and Trematon Castle on the north and Antony House on the south side of the river all lie within a few miles of each other and once the families living there visited each other by river. All these houses may be seen to their best advantage from the water.

Ince Castle, a castellated house, is the property of the Boyd family who moved to Cornwall about twenty-five years ago and have done much to restore some of the riverside properties including Ince, Shillingham and Wivelscombe. The house of Ince was originally built for the Killigrew family and is constructed of a pinky brick with four slate towers and castellations. It is at the end of a narrow promontory with the river rising at high tide on all sides.

Trematon Castle rides high on a hill above the river and the Forder creek. Though it is a Norman castle it is believed there may have been some sort of earlier fortification there. The Doomsday Book records that the local Norman lord, Reginald de Valletort, held it for Robert of Mortain, Earl of Cornwall and half brother of William the Conqueror.

The view from the castle of the tidal reaches of the lower Tamar make it a good vantage point for defence as enemies often threatened from the Tamar or Lynher. The curtain wall and the keep are the oldest parts of the castle, the beautiful gatehouse being added by Earl Edmund of Cornwall at the end of the thirteenth century.

The Black Prince, first Duke of Cornwall, is said to have stayed at the castle on several occasions and the property belongs to the Duchy of Cornwall to this day.

There has long been speculation that Sir Francis Drake hid some of his treasure there; some say there may still be some buried in a cave but nothing has ever been found.

In 1600 Carew wrote in his *Survey of Cornwall*:

Trematon Castle rides high on a hill above the river and Antony Passage.

'. . . all the inner buildings falleth daily into ruin and decay and only there remains the ivy tapposed walls and a good dwelling for the keeper and his gaol.'

It was Benjamin Tucker, appointed Surveyor General of the Duchy of Cornwall in 1808, who built a house within the castle walls and destroyed several feet of the wall to give the house a finer view over the river. It seems incredible that he ever got away with the destruction of the ancient stone walls, but he did, and three generations of Tuckers lived in the house and enjoyed the marvellous setting. Hundreds of people would travel up the river in Victorian times to view the house from the water, including Queen Victoria herself.

Twenty two years ago my parents went to live at Trematon, taking a long lease from the Duchy of Cornwall. I can still remember going to see the house and castle for the first time and finding the setting almost unbelievable. From every window of the house were views of the castle walls and the river

It was Benjamin Tucker who built a house within the castle walls at Trematon.

beyond, with great battleships lying in the Hamoaze. Beyond could be seen the town of Plymouth, spread out like a map in the distance.

It has one of the happiest atmospheres of any house and grounds that I have ever known. None of the harshness and battles that took place in the grounds, or the terrible atrocities that were committed when it was a gaol in Carew's time, seem to have lingered there. The keep, in its simple splendour, sits above the house and I often marvelled that I could lie in my bath and look at it. Each year, it seemed appropriate that kestrels used to nest in the keep walls. I often wondered if they had been coming there since the eleventh century.

The other most famous Cornish castles—Restormel, Launceston and Tintagel—all have a fine quality, but Benjamin Tucker's daring in taking down part of the curtain wall and building a house in the midst of the castle made one of the most unusual and pleasant dwellings that one could hope to know.

Two years ago my parents left the house and it is now cared for with equal love by Mr and Mrs Ian Rennie and their family. The castle is open to the public for charity two or three times in the year.

The grand house on the other side of the river from Trematon is Antony, home of the Carew family since the fifteenth century, when the manor of Antony was inherited by Alexander Carew. Carew's *Survey of Cornwall* is one of the most used and admired reference books in Cornwall and was written by Richard Carew who was born at Antony House in 1555. The *Survey* was originally printed in 1602, twice reprinted in the eighteenth century and then in a volume in 1811. Thanks to F. E. Halliday we have a newly edited edition published this century.

F. E. Halliday begins his introduction to the volume he edited with this paragraph: 'In the south-east angle of Cornwall, the little River Lynher suddenly turns east, and shortly before joining the severing water of the Tamar, expands into an estuary. Where it thus turns and broadens, the church and village of Antony cling to the slope of a hill close to its southern shore, and some two miles downstream, to the left of the highway to Torpoint and Plymouth, is Antony House. It is a fine classical building of Pentewan stone in the style of Gibbs, erected in 1721, and from its terrace, beyond the lawns and woods there is a noble prospect of the river, on the other side of which is the ruined keep of Trematon Castle, backed by the northern hills . . . It was here that Richard Carew was born on July 17th 1555.'

It is nice to compare this with Carew's own description in his Survey: 'Passing somewhat further up you meet with the foot of the Lynher where it winneth fellowship with Tamar, that till then, and this yet longer, retaining their names though their over-weak streams were long before confounded by the predominant salt water. A little within this mouth of Lynher standeth East Antony, the poor home of mine ancestors, with which in this manner they were invested.'

Carew loved Cornwall, was considered a learned man, taking much time for his reading, learning of languages and his later *Survey of Cornwall*, but his favourite form of relaxation was to work on the 'fishful pond'. He wrote a poem about it and spent many hours constructing it and stocking it with fish. He loved the Lynher too and wrote at least two poems about the river which flowed past his house.

The house is now owned by the National Trust and is open to the public in season, but it is good to know that a family of Carews still live there.

Opposite Antony House lies the village of Antony Passage. For hundreds of years the busy ferry was operated from here, and in the deep waters of the river loading of roadstone and the produce of the surrounding quarries took place from barges to schooners.

The Crossley family for generations ran the ferry and the mill and they held the fishing rights for netting salmon. Later the Chapman family married into the Crossley family and the two families have been the mainstay of this riverside crossing for the last century. People still say that you cannot live happily at Antony unless you have their permission.

The tide mill at Antony Passage – a memorial to the time when the river was a working place.

An earlier railway line running above Antony Passage.

The rowing regattas were a great annual event along this part of the river estuary and the Crossleys and Chapmans always took part, often winning these events which drew great crowds and were most hotly and determinedly contested. This regatta was open to women as well as men and Grandma Doris Chapman is the proud winner of some silver cups for her rowing efforts.

Doris Chapman now lives at Forder village and is 81 years old but she remembers with great clarity many stories of the river and especially of the years when she was running the rowing ferry boat herself during the second world war for Sir Reginald Pole-Carew. She was paid a £1 a week and the ferry fare was one penny — twopence on Sundays.

She remembers two particular near-disasters when the horse boat was in use. Once a whole flock of

sheep was washed overboard on the rising tide and had to be picked up further upriver where they were luckily all found safe and sound. On another occasion she remembers the ferry boat going across to Torpoint to pick up a coffin for burial at St Stephen's Church, near Saltash. Once again the tide was rising fast and this time the coffin was swept overboard by an unexpected wave. The boat was rowed in hot pursuit and eventually the coffin was reclaimed on board. Some trouble was taken to drain the water from the coffin, but apparently when it was brought into the church and lifted at the altar, to the congregation's amazement, streams of water gushed from the coffin.

When Doris Chapman (née Crossley) went to Antony Passage, she was three months old and her father ran the ferry and they lived at Ferry House Inn. Her great grandfather before had run the pub at

Antony Passage. Doris was one of nine children. At eighteen she met her husband, Elwyn Chapman, who was in the navy and it is most appropriate that they met in the middle of the river while Doris was rowing.

Her son, Ron Chapman, has three sons who have all taken a keen interest in the rowing regattas and Neil Chapman, Doris's grandson, told me that in one year he and his brothers entered 31 regattas. They were an unbeatable team for several years. Neil told me that when he was eleven years old he challenged his grandmother to a rowing race 'and she licked me'.

Mr and Mrs Ron Chapman now live in a modern house above Antony Passage where once the railway line ran and the view across the water to the Royal Naval training point, where many of their rowing boats are moored, is quite magnificent.

In the old days a man just had to stand on the other side of the water at Jupiter Point and wave a white handkerchief for the ferryman to row across and pick him up. At that time every single house at Antony was owned by Antony Estate and lived in by a Crossley or a Chapman.

Now the tide mill below the beautiful stone viaduct is just a memorial to the time when the river was a working place. The ferry house and pub no longer retain their original purpose but Mr Chapman's family still go out to net the salmon below the villages of Sheviock and Antony in the season which lasts from 2 March to 31 August.

Perhaps the Lynher River has more indigenous Cornish people living along its banks than any of the other Cornish rivers. So many of the beautiful riverside places have become retreats for people who have made them their second homes or come here to retire. There is nothing wrong with this, it is nice to know that people appreciate the secluded riverside places, but much of the character of the countryside will be lost if those who work there and take part in the community are not living there as well.

I still find any sort of continuity in the villages and towns and estates of Cornwall a comforting notion.

Whether it be the Chapmans and the Crossleys at Antony Passage who have piloted ships along the narrow reaches of the river, fished for salmon, loaded and transported stone from all the neighbouring quarries and carried passengers to and fro across the river for generations, or the Eliots or the Carews who have survived in their inherited estates but given back to the community in the same way that they have taken, there is something reassuring about people belonging to one place and their families continuing to do so.

The River Fal

Each of the six rivers in this book has come to mean something particular to me. In the case of the Fal it is Peace.

Maybe this is because it is the only river on which I have actually spent the night. It was in early summer, on a day of brilliant sunshine, that a friend took us out on his boat from Falmouth Harbour. We stopped to admire St Mawes Castle and the protected cove of St Mawes itself, and then wended our way past the opening to Restronguet Creek and the great house of Trelissick, the grounds of which are so impressive from both land and water. On we went past that ancient river crossing of King Harry Ferry where huge sea-going vessels are laid up, and then gazed up to Tregothnan and the parkland around, finally anchoring on a peaceful bend of the river where only the sound of birds disturbed a perfect silence.

In the last evening glow we sat on deck watching the gold and pink sky colour the water until it seemed lit from within. We even talked in whispers in case we damaged the silence. The sense of peacefulness that surrounded us was so calming that it seemed to wipe the slate clean; all petty worries slipped away so that just sitting and appreciating our surroundings became a sort of confession, a return to innocence.

The great wooded banks rose above us and they

'I went to talk to a great river boatman, Jim Morrison, who has worked on the Fal all his life . . .'

turned golden, too, in the last mellow light of late evening. At the river's edge, heavy branches touched the water of the rising tide and over on a bank a heron sat hunched waiting for his fish.

It was an experience I shall never forget. That night it was the 'slip slop' of the water and the otherwise deep silence that lulled us to sleep in our bunks. We slept like children who did not have to tangle with the problems of a modern and adult world and the necessity to worry about them was abolished. Life would go on, the good and the bad would vie for prominence, but there it seemed certain, without a shadow of doubt, that good would always predominate. It was great to be alive and in that place of beauty.

That night as I lay in my bunk I could still feel the gentleness of our surroundings.

In the morning the light was bright and fresh and new, the river misty in its beauty, and the peacefulness still just as apparent. With gusto we sat on deck and

Ruan Creek: 'The sense of peacefulness that surrounded us was so calming . . .'

ate breakfast of bacon and eggs. From the middle of the river each way we turned seemed more beautiful.

The Fal has come to mean many things to many people. Some of the most beautiful and lush country-side in Cornwall surrounds it and yet it was not always as peaceful as it was to us that night, for the Fal was a working river and a man with a boat could always earn his living when goods were transported on the waterways.

I went to talk to a great river boatman called Jim Morrison who has worked on the Fal all his life and knows it, not so much as a peaceful river, but one that must be understood and navigated in difficult tides and currents.

Jim Morrison was brought up on barges. If there was work to be done and father needed him Jim would take a day off school. He can proudly claim to have worked a lifetime under sail and says, 'I have discharged every sort of vessel you can think of though most times, nowadays, it is taking a few friends out for a day on the river'. He has worked on stone barges, quay punts and oyster dredgers. He was also for a time the skipper of the river barge, *Shamrock*, which has been restored and is now kept at Cotehele Quay on the Tamar.

He has taken stone up the Helford River to Port Navas and Gweek returning in the dark of night. He has sold coal at Helford, at that time costing £2 a ton, and he and his father would hire two horses and a cart to deliver the coal to local farmers. 'It cost eight shillings a day to hire the horse and cart,' he told me when I talked to him at his house in Falmouth.

He was eleven years old when he started going about in boats regularly on a Truro river barge called *Swift*. In 1928 they lost that vessel at Stack Point just south west of Falmouth and then he bought another boat called *Eclipse*. At that time the stone trade was growing and so Jim was soon fully involved with carrying stone up river. He says he has always liked the Fal River — 'rather more atmosphere than most', he told me.

The men who worked on boats at Falmouth know all the rivers and creeks in the area like the back of their hands. There are seven rivers that empty their waters into the sea at Carrick Roads and endless little hidden waterways. In Carrick Roads the wrecks of fifty ships are said to lie, conquered by gales over the years since the eighteenth century.

Jim told me that he can remember people still sailing as far as Devoran up Restronguet Creek but this silted up by the 1920s. Tin was mined at Devoran in the earlier part of the nineteenth century.

Then Jim explained to me that the Fal was once navigable as far as Tregony and how much work once went on along that waterway. There are so many creeks and inlets in the complicated waterway of the mouth of the Fal that only a man who has spent many years working and living there can fully appreciate and understand where the quays and deep channels lie.

Before I left Falmouth I accompanied Jim to his favourite pub, the Chainlocker, where so many boatmen and sailors still gather. Here amidst the camaraderie of seafaring men you realize that these men are known by the boats and vessels that they have owned or worked over the years; they are admired for their seagoing skills and for the stories they have to tell about river and sea voyages.

Jim explained to me that the Fal was once navigable as far as Tregony.

It was like seeing into a foreign world which held great enticements but in which one could not really partake without also understanding the language of men who have worked boats.

It is a far cry from the language of people who just muck about in boats; these men have made their living, often under dangerous circumstances, in their barges and ketches, and they understand more about the workings of tidal waters than they ever could about motorways or computers. You feel their skill was almost bred into them, and therefore is easier to admire and appreciate than those skills which have been taught or learned from books. Often their instinct is more valuable than any knowledge. Being with Jim and being introduced to his friends was a real privilege, an expansion to my horizons. I felt I had met with a whole new breed of skilled men whom I had not properly appreciated before.

It was on Jim's instructions that I went for one of the most beautiful drives in the world, following the River Fal. I had my niece with me and it helped to have a map reader for we were bent on following all the minor roads, discovering new places as we went. We turned down a road leading to the river by the great house of Trelissick. Trelissick, as I have mentioned before, has some of the most beautiful gardens and grounds in Cornwall. It is a perfect setting and has one of the finest views of the Fal River. John Betjeman describes it as 'the swell house of Trelissick remodelled by P. F. Robinson 1824-25 in the Grecian style'. The gardens are owned by the National Trust and open to the public. It is in the grounds of this house that the modern home for the Bishop of Truro has been built.

As we wended our way down to the river we came to the little village of Feock. It is enchanting, especially on a clear spring day as it was when we found it. There was a man thatching one of the cottage roofs opposite the little church which is well-known for its detached tower. It is said that the last sermon in the Cornish language was preached here. It is the setting of the village that is so pretty with the river glimpsed here and there between gaps in hedges or buildings or gravestones and the church so tranquil, its graveyard on a little promontory reaching out into the river.

Below: The Eclipse, *a ketch rigged trading vessel owned by the Morrisons of Falmouth in the 1930s. Above: Their boat, Mayflower, sailing back from oyster dredging.*

Cornish Shrimpers beached during their 1984 regatta in Channals Creek on the River Fal below Trelissick House.

Nearby, I am told, the film of *Treasure Island* was made, in one of the hidden yet beautifully situated coves called Loe Beach, but we followed the road around until we came down the steep hill to King Harry Ferry.

I never cease to get a shock on seeing the number and size of the cargo vessels which are anchored just off the ferry crossing point. There is something horribly sad and yet impressive about them. Will there ever be the work for these merchant vessels that there once was? Or will they also become redundant like the river barges that carried so much of the farm produce, quarried stone and mined minerals to their destination? The water here at Turnaware Point as it is called has a minimum depth of sixty feet even at low tide. There have been as many as thirty cargo vessels lying at anchor at this point.

When you cross on the little ferry—named after Henry VI who is reputed to have stayed nearby—the ships tower above you, dwarfing all around them, and they look so unkempt and forgotten.

One day, when I was crossing on the ferry, I watched as they manoeuvred one of the great ships down river. There were two or three tugs pulling her, and one little motorboat that busily made its way round and round the vessels to see that all was going well. It seemed quite impossible that the ship would ever find her way past her compatriots into the wide harbour beyond. I imagine she did, otherwise we would have heard about it.

Once on the other side of the Fal we did not need to be told that we were in the Roseland Peninsula, the garden of Cornwall as it is called. H. V. Morton described this subtropical landscape: 'I have blundered into a Garden of Eden that cannot be described with pen and paint.' People who think that Cornwall is

Above: King Harry Ferry. Below: Laid-up tankers. 'There have been as many as thirty cargo vessels lying at anchor at Turnaware Point just below the ferry.'

made up of stark and harsh country with nothing but rocks and tors, heather and bracken to her name should visit this part of the county. It is almost overwhelmingly pretty with its winding high lanes and sudden flashes of the river below.

Once again, trying to find the lesser-known parts of the Roseland, I took a lane which led me into the village of Philleigh with its beautiful church and popular pub. As I drove on and took a right turning I passed a house which was so eye-catching I stopped and backed up. Through the gate it stood, so surprising in its stark elegance, nothing pretty about this house. It was handsome. It was slate faced with a slightly overgrown driveway and a solid straightforwardness to it. A sign invited us in for tea and cakes. The invitation was irresistible though we were not hungry or thirsty, just dying of curiosity.

The house was once the old rectory and it had the feeling of such an abode: high ceilings with elaborate mouldings; slightly worn and yet comfortably furnished rooms with open fireplaces. It is now called the Glebe Country House and is open through winter and summer for paying guests. Part of the house is Queen Anne with lower ceilings and huge beams, the rest Georgian. The earlier date of building is 1660. There was something haunting about the house, as we sat, my niece and I alone in the huge dining room, and ate home-baked scones and lashings of Cornish cream. It was as if the house stood apart from the whitewashed prettiness of the rest of the village, and was proud of being different and yet part of a village mentioned in the Doomsday Book.

Whatever it was that was special about the house I will not forget the excitement at so unexpectedly catching sight of it through the gate posts which we so nearly passed by.

Cornwall, and particularly riverside Cornwall, is often full of unexpected surprises. You drive through high hedges, along tiny winding lanes full of ferns, primroses, pink campion, bluebells, meadow sweet, or bracken, depending on the season and often, unless you watch with care, you will miss fleeting glimpses through a gateway or a gap in the hedge.

We made our way up river to Ruan Lanihorne, wanting to experience the quayside once so full of

Left: The Glebe Country House at Philleigh. 'A sign invited us in for tea and cakes.'
Below: Feock Church with its separate tower.

activity in the working days of sail. It is another of Cornwall's quiet creeks. On the quay stone it reads: 'Presented to the parishioners of Ruan Lanihorne by Mrs C. Hyde, 1919.'

Not far from here in the eighteenth century a huge coffin, measuring 11 foot 3 inches long, was unearthed by tin miners. Could it have belonged to a Cornish giant?

There is a little bridge at Ruan Lanihorne where you can cross the creek and look across the wide open space of water and then the road climbs steeply up through some of the most lovely woods I have driven through, Lamorran Woods. We followed this lovely drive down past Lamorran itself with farm buildings and a church which seemed untouched by time, a dead-end little hamlet right by the river, and then realized that we were skirting the established grounds of Tregothnan, the home of Lord Falmouth.

You keep crossing the drive ways leading to the house which give fine vistas in the winter when the marvellous woods of ash and beech and oak are not in full leaf.

St Michael-in-Penkevil is another hamlet in the shadow of the great house of Tregothnan and in the church of Pentewan stone there is a window designed by William Morris, Rosetti and Burne Jones. The church is originally thirteenth-century and restored by G. E. Street in 1862. There are many monuments to the Boscawen family.

Below: The Fal at its source.   Right: Near its beginnings at Indian Queens.

You join the main road again at Tresillian and see the great drive to the house which I am told winds on for four miles. The gateway was designed by Wilkins who also built the house of Tregothnan in 1815.

The little church at Tresillian always fascinates me and reminds me more of a church building in Mexico than in a Cornish village. This slice of land belonging to the Boscawen family seems to guard the turning of the river and, brooding all around, looks down to many of the quieter spots on the Fal.

If you follow the main road from Truro to St Austell, the Fal valley widens and becomes the farming parish of Creed. Creed itself was the church town of Grampound. The Fal river runs through the slate-housed village of Grampound—*grand pont*; 'great bridge' seems a rather exaggerated description of this crossing of the Fal river. It always·seems to me a particularly Cornish town and many of the most ardent preservers of all the best Cornish traditions come from this part of Cornwall.

Grampound is of particular interest as being one of the rotten boroughs. For nearly three hundred years between fifty and sixty electors at Grampound managed to send two members to the House of Commons, but the voters of Grampound got a reputation for asking high prices for their services, rejecting the Edgcumbes of Cotehele as nominators of the members. They found they had better remuneration from Lord Eliot of St Germans, a professional borough broker.

The Fal at Grampound.

Mylor Church overlooking the river.

Then they changed to another patriot. So it went on until Grampound became a byword for corruption in an already corrupt world. In 1821 an act was passed which disenfranchised Grampound and then the bartering came to an end.

It is fascinating to realize that at the beginning of the nineteenth century Cornwall had 21 boroughs and sent 44 members to the House of Commons. In fact in 1831 Cornwall and Wiltshire sent more members to Parliament than Yorkshire, Lancashire, Warwickshire, Middlesex, Worcestershire and Somerset combined.

The upper reaches of the Fal offer many unspoilt and beautiful views and all these places are linked by the river which ends at the beautiful harbour town of Falmouth.

This town was originally a mere village dominated by the nearby town of Penryn which now takes second place. Falmouth was once known as Smithick, reputed to come from the fact that there was a smith's forge on the creek, and then became known as Pennycomequick, which probably derived from the Celtic *Pen-y-cum*, 'head of the vale'. It was not until the seventeenth century that the Killigrew family constructed a quay at Falmouth and the maritime business began to grow.

The golden age of Falmouth came with the Falmouth Packets, a post office system under sail, which lasted from 1688 to 1850. The brave sailing boats not only carried mail and parcels around the coast and overseas but they were also the only means of conveying money for business purposes, so they carried gold and were open to all kinds of dangers from the privateers of the time. At one time forty packet ships undertook about a hundred voyages each year from Falmouth.

It was the steam ships and the railway which brought an end to the mail business at Falmouth when it was transferred to Southampton and Liverpool.

Smugglers abounded everywhere and a Customs and Excise Office was built to try and deal with this problem as early as 1652, before the town received its charter in 1660, but local people and outsiders continued with these practices and it proved difficult to control the illegal importation of all kinds of goods.

The docks at Falmouth.

The castles of Pendennis and St Mawes were in fact built during the time of Henry VIII for defence of Penryn, which was then the major town, against the French marauders who so plagued the Cornish coast at that time. There they stand as sentinels to the harbour of Falmouth which has over so many years afforded comfort and sanctuary to sea-weary men and their vessels.

Falmouth is a town of views, built tightly on a hill, with narrow winding streets, full of atmosphere, and I am always struck by the friendliness of the place. You walk from shop to shop, and see local people stopping to talk to each other. Out of season it is as if everyone knows everyone else, be they seamen or businessmen, shopowners or hoteliers.

One of the great sights of the town is the long narrow steps that wend their way down several hundred feet named, appropriately enough, Jacob's ladder.

In Falmouth I am often reminded of the comment of Anne Treneer in her book *School House in the Wind*. 'In my arrogance I had thought of Falmouth (God forgive me) as a place for "visitors" and to be avoided. But when towards sunset I stood on the rocks below the lighthouse, facing the harbour, I knew that everthing that had ever been written about the beauty of Falmouth Harbour was true.'

The town of Falmouth itself. 'Falmouth is a town of views, built tightly on a hill . . .'

Tom McClean arriving at Falmouth in 1982 in Giltspur, at 9 foot 9 inches long, the smallest boat to have crossed the Atlantic. To regain the record, he later cut a full 2 feet off the stern of Giltspur.

The Tamar River

The River Tamar is a grand river and its greatest claim to fame is that it forms almost the entire border between Devon and Cornwall. If it were not for a few short miles of land between the source of the river and the north coast cliffs, Cornwall would be an island bound on three sides by the sea and the fourth by the Tamar.

The feeling of Cornwall being a land apart is perpetuated by the Cornish people; they do not like being classed as English. 'Crossing the water to England' is a phrase still used by people who venture into Devon across the watery dividing line.

The river wends its way from the north down past the handsome town of Launceston, with its magnificent Norman hill-top castle of Dunheved and ornately carved granite church, through wide water meadows, under fifteenth-century bridges and between high cliffs. Then, near the riverside village of Gunnislake, it becomes tidal and interwoven with the busy life of mining which dominated the last reaches of the Tamar in the eighteenth century, and which came to such an abrupt halt at the beginning of this.

More tin, copper, silver and arsenic were mined in the region than anywhere else in Europe. The great chimneys belched smoke, the earth was scarred by the ever-deepening mines and the mine engines and water

An unusual house in Calstock.

Morwellham, now a museum, was once busy with boats loading the produce of the mines of the area.

Above: 'If you watch the fishermen netting for salmon at Halton Quay, it is as if time has stood still . . .' Left: A pleasure trip up the Tamar.

wheels could be heard for miles around as well as the bells which called the change of shifts. Gunnislake, Morwellham and Calstock were thriving places peopled by men and women who made their living from the mines.

When the end of the mining came it was sudden. The valley towns became ghost towns as the men, knowing no other trade or skill, travelled overseas to gain employment. It was often said, and still is, that there was not a mine in the world where you would not find a Cornishman at work.

The Duke of Bedford was the great landowner around the Gunnislake district where the Devon Great Consuls mine was worked. He did well from the mining boom, had a reputation for housing and caring for his tenants far better than many landlords of the time, but was obviously thankful when the mining was all over for he was quick to re-landscape much of the mutilated earth, happily returning it to the wildlife and agricultural uses.

If you take a trip up the Tamar River by boat or land, you cannot miss the many monuments to that period. The tilting mine stacks, the evidence of canals, the old railway lines, the quays and wharves built to take huge cargoes, and the remnants of mills and engines.

Some of the buildings have been destroyed or crumbled to nothing through the years. It is hard to imagine that on the Cornish banks of Gunnislake, right by Newbridge, there was once a five storey building which was a miners' hostel and ale house incorporated.

Nearby the Bealswood brickworks gave another form of employment. It was a vast complex in the early part of the century using local blue clay to make the bricks. There was also quarrying in the area, at Hingston Down and way up on Kit Hill with its

panoramic views of the Tamar, and nearer the river at Pearson's Quarry at Gunnislake. This quarry was worked from 1808 to 1914 and its workings were over 130 feet deep. From this quarry stone was used to build Dover Harbour, Devonport Dockyard, Blackfriars Bridge and to pave many of London's streets. Like the mines it was closed with little warning; by then its owner was a millionaire but as many as seven hundred men were without employment.

It is hard to imagine today the impact this had on the community. People were often living in terrible conditions, a man and his wife and nine children being reported, in one case, as inhabiting a two-roomed cottage with very little furnishing and only straw for bedding. So much has changed in the last hundred years, and contrary to popular opinion, some things have changed for the better.

One of the practices that has not changed a great deal is that of the licensed fishermen who net for salmon, except in earlier days the fish were much more plentiful. Today if you watch the men netting for salmon at Cotehele Quay or Halton Quay it is as if time has stood still, for the method has hardly changed over the years. It is a beautiful and graceful sight to watch, though hard work, for the men slowly let out the nets from rowing boats and then quickly haul them in again, hoping to find a fat fish or two to swell the coffers.

Having lived for some years on the Cornish banks of the Tamar River, and watched it in its many moods, glinting in the valley below the house, I have learned to love it well and to be enthralled with the history of the valley and the changes wrought along the banks within living memory.

The lifestyle of the people who lived along all the rivers of Cornwall has changed considerably in the last century, but none seem to have changed to quite the extent as that of the people of the Tamar valley. What is so fascinating is that the older people can remember with such clarity a way of life that is so

Horsebridge on the Tamar.

Looking from Bere Alston towards Cotehele.

completely different to that which we experience today.

For there are people living in the valley who remember the days when the lime kilns were still in use by the waterside, when water mills turned to grind corn and cut wood, when the fields with their intricate strip cultivation were filled to overflowing with the bulbs, flowers, fruits and vegetables of the famous market gardens. These gardens were as much a part of the district as the mining and some of them survive today.

I have listened to stories of sailing boats and barges coming way up river to discharge their cargoes of fertilisers, grain and corn, timber and stone. River traffic may have been depleted by the coming of the railway and road traffic but it still went on well into this century.

Many of those who have grown up along the banks of the Tamar spent their time as children travelling up and down river by rowing boat and little time on the roads. They remember well making weekly trips with their mothers to Devonport where produce from the land was sold at market stalls, and they always travelled by boat.

The horse was then still the mainstay of all heavy duties on the land, or for conveying heavy loads from the waterways to the inland market towns. I have spoken to men who talk lyrically of working with the heavy horses, walking miles in one day of ploughing, but receiving a special kind of satisfaction from the close relationship they developed with their working partners. Some of them tell me they would give anything for a day behind a horse and plough.

They remember too goading their horses behind wagons as they ferried their heavy loads up the almost perpendicular hills of the valley, sometimes needing a team of four to reach the more even terrain of the higher roads.

The fine viaduct at Calstock.

In the fields of the Tamar valley thick white blossom flowered each spring. It transformed the landscape. The famous cherry trees, many of them grafted there and given names of local places and people, were such a sight that people would travel from miles to see them and later taste their sweet fruit.

Picking the cherries was usually the responsibility of the women and children. When the children were still young they coped with the lower branches and the women could be seen, dressed in their long skirts, up the forty rung ladders which were specially built in the area, picking the fruit all day long, before the birds could get to them.

Flowers had to be picked while they were still in bud and so little huts were erected here and there where the bunching could take place in the early hours of the morning. Some of these bunching houses still stand, dilapidated, nearly all unused, but a reminder of those times past when all hands were busy whether they belonged to men, women or children. In fact the children's help was sorely needed and they would often take a day off from school to help with the fruit and flower picking. Fruit pickers came from miles around to help with the work, living in the sheds of farmers during the week and returning home only at weekends.

If you drive down to the last tidal reaches of the Tamar River, it is difficult to imagine all the variety of work that once abounded there, and now has totally vanished. Only a comparatively small area of land is still used for flower growing; the cherries have nearly gone although some young preservers of the past are hoping to graft some of the old types of cherry and replant them in the valley. The mining has, of course, totally vanished. The river traffic is of a different nature, no working boats passing now except those of the salmon fishermen. Miners' cottages have been converted to make pretty retirement homes, or for those commuting to Plymouth or Tavistock.

An idyllic spot on the Tamar.

Picking cherries in long skirts early this century in the market gardens of the Tamar Valley.

If you sit by the old coal store at Halton Quay which has been converted to make a little chapel you can imagine the sound of the mine bells calling the change of shift, you can sense the urgency that once existed when every service was offered within a community.

There were carpenters, tailors, wheelwrights, shoemakers, blacksmiths and breweries, dressmakers, butchers and bakers, even in the smaller villages. Now that none of these services are offered in country communities it is not difficult to understand the growing unemployment figures, or the need for men to travel to their work, sometimes several miles.

There is, however, still enough market gardening going on to give the patterned strips to the land. I have recently seen a man sowing his seed by hand, like some Biblical picture, as he walked the steep slopes that lead down to the wide river.

Because it is always easy to let the mind wander back in time in Cornwall, so it is easy to imagine the past, much further back than a century ago. The Celtic saints came to this beautiful waterside country over a thousand years ago as they did to so many of the riverside places in Cornwall and just above Halton Quay there is a holy well where St Intract, son of an Irish king, and his sister St Dominica came and made a hermitage. You feel that holy Celtic touch at Halton Quay. An old gentleman I know once told me that whenever he felt low in spirit he would go, in the evening light, and sit by the water there, and would soon feel renewed by the atmosphere and the view.

The grandest and best known house on the River Tamar must be the medieval house of Cotehele, once the home of the Mount Edgcumbe family and now owned by the National Trust.

It is built on a hill above the river with the gardens, full of rare shrubs and trees, sloping down to the water in a dramatic way. It may be the situation of the house which gives it its special atmosphere but it certainly is one of the most visited of the National Trust houses in Cornwall.

Cotehele is small enough, and intimate enough, to have retained its feeling of a home lived in and loved. The hall with its white-washed walls all hung with armour, the wooden floors, the beautiful tapestries

The Tamar begins to widen out as it enters the lower reaches.

*This handsome piebald duck, the Shelduck, is
quite numerous on the Tamar and Lynher rivers.*

Mallard ducklings are always cute, but few survive to adulthood.

which hang in room after room, the four-poster beds and the materials with which they are draped, all contrive to make this a house of unique beauty.

The house came to the Mount Edgcumbe family through marriage to an heiress – Hilaria Cotehele in 1353. It stayed the property of the Mount Edgcumbe family until the estate was handed over to the National Trust through the Treasury as part payment of death duties by the 6th Earl of Mount Edgcumbe in 1947. Cotehele was the first historic country house and estate to be acquired by the Trust in this way.

All the family furniture, tapestries and armour were left on loan to the Trust in the house until they were in turn given to the Trust by the Treasury which had accepted them in lieu of estate duty on the death of the 6th Earl.

The continuity of furnishings and of owners has somehow affected the place. It is loved as much by local people who walk through the gardens and along the riverside walks as it is by the tourists who come to sample its attractions.

The Mill House of Cotehele and the quayside have also been restored and kept much as they were when they were in working order. And down by the quay the old river barge, the *Shamrock*, is moored, having been restored by the Trust and the Maritime Trust. It is a fine sight to see this handsome vessel moored by the quay buildings where so much work once went on. And because of the little museum that has been set up in one of the buildings it is easy to understand exactly the nature of the activities that took place from this busy centre of the Tamar valley.

I was lucky enough to meet Mrs Marie Martin some years ago. She was brought up at the Mill House at Cotehele, her father being the last miller. She has many happy memories of the atmosphere of the valley when it was a hive of activity with people bringing trees from the woods to be sawn at the mill, grain arriving on barges similar to the *Shamrock*, and goods being brought by horse and cart. She remembers it as a very happy childhood with so much going on around them.

Her youngest daughter, Mary Martin, is now known as the Tamar Valley painter. She attended the Royal Academy School, travelled in Europe, but eventually came home to the valley where she lives in a little house perched in the trees above the Mill of Cotehele. She is truly part of the valley, does not like to paint anywhere else, and can often be seen, easel in hand wandering through the lanes and fields of the area.

Her paintings have been exhibited in London, Bristol and Plymouth, and in many venues in Cornwall and Devon, and she has reproduced over and

The Author at Halton Quay.

Mary Martin, the painter, and James Armstrong-Evans. Preservers of the past – they have grafted many of the old fruit trees of the Tamar Valley.

over again with the greatest feeling and expertise the beauties of the valley that she loves so well.

She is also extremely tied up with preserving some of the best of the old customs. She and another enthusiast, James Armstrong-Evans, have worked together through the last few years to graft some of the old types of cherry in the district that were fast dying out. Because of their research they have revived and written down many of the old names of the fifteen different kinds of Tamar valley cherries which were once so famous and so popular.

There is Burcombe and Birchenhayes called after

Mary Martin is known as the Tamar Valley painter. Here she captures the beauty of the Valley she loves so well.

farms in the area, there are Smith's Smutz, Jan Jane, Grylls and Steers Black all linked with names of people who have worked in the valley.

Their enthusiasm for the revival of the old cherries has received encouragement from the people of the valley and from the National Trust and they hope to plant some of the trees in one of the old orchards adjoining Cotehele.

They and their friends who are interested in retaining some of the old occupations have also revived the art of cider making in an old cider press which is still intact, near Callington. I have watched these young people at work with the horse pulling the heavy granite wheel which crushes the apples and the intricate skill that goes into plaiting the straw to make the cheese into which the apple pulp is placed and squashed firmly for its juice.

It is a wonderfully communal act, and one which brings back the old practice of neighbour helping neighbour. I think of all the things that have died out in the Tamar valley this is the practice most missed. Only fifty years ago all the working people relied on one another in some way to make their lives possible and fruitful. Each man took it as a matter of course that he would help his neighbour during the busy times. Even when they buried their dead, they would help carry the coffins from household to churchyard through the narrow, steep, winding lanes. Now it is not that strange to find that people living next door to one another do not know each other, and are afraid of being considered interfering if they venture too close.

Cornwall has often produced eccentrics and taken them to its heart. One such eccentric built the fine house of Pentillie Castle with its marvellous situation on a hill overlooking the Tamar further down river from Cotehele and Halton Quay.

It was built by James Tillie, an ex-steward of the Coryton family and strangely, it was the Coryton family who later, through marriage, inherited the house and who still own Pentillie Castle and estate which stretches down to the Halton area.

Mr Tillie commanded that when he died his body should be placed at the top of Mount Ararat, a

'The Tamar is a grand river.'

wooded hill opposite the house, along with his pipe and his port. His body had a more conventional grave but there is still a statue of him on the hilltop.

The house was originally built in the seventeenth century, but it is believed that there had been an earlier habitation and perhaps a chapel on the site. In 1810 major alterations were done to the house by W. Wilkins, the famous architect of that time.

In more recent years the house was completely renovated, many of the later additions done away

The Franklin's gull which spent part of the winter on the Tamar and attracted large numbers of birdwatchers from all over Britain.

*The white-**rumped** sandpiper.*

Coots breed along the riverbanks and reservoirs of the Westcountry. They appear harmless but will sometimes kill the young of other birds.

with, and the present simple and classical style is more akin with the original building and very beautiful.

The Coryton family lived at 'Newton Ferrers', a fine house above the Lynher River, now owned by Sir Valentine Abdy; they then moved to the manor house of Cracadon also in the Tamar valley and finally came to Pentillie in 1770 where they have remained ever since.

Much of the market gardening land on their estate has been put back to forestry, but in between the trees can still be seen the serried ranks of daffodils and narcissi.

Pentillie Castle lies on the last great bend of the protected Tamar valley—beyond lie the villages of Cargreen and Landulph—and then the river joins the sea beyond the town of Saltash.

Here the two great bridges span the Tamar, the main crossing point now between Devon and Cornwall. The famous railway bridge designed by Isambard Kingdom Brunel and opened by Prince Albert in 1859 lies parallel with the more modern toll road bridge and the lines of the two bridges contrast nicely if you stand down by the river below them. Before either of these bridges were built an ancient ferry ran travellers between the Devon and Cornish banks. The ferry is documented as early as the thirteenth century but was in existence long before

Children wait on the Cornish banks of the Tamar to cross on the ferry to Plymouth.

that. It once belonged to the Manor of Trematon and in 1356 the Black Prince, the first Duke of Cornwall and Lord of Trematon, rewarded his porter William Lenche for his good service at the Battle of Poitiers by giving him the lease for life of the Passage of Saltash.

Now that the bridges have taken over the duty of transferring all forms of transportation across this ancient river crossing, the sense of timelessness has gone from the banks of Saltash town. In fact Saltash is in danger of being taken over as a dormitory town for those who work in Plymouth, but it does retain some of its ancient character and its older inhabitants are proud to claim that Saltash is a far older town than that of Plymouth.

I never cross the bridge at Saltash without appreciating the grandness of this last aspect of the River Tamar. I like to think of the river's beginnings, wending its way under Indulgence bridges and through calm water meadows where fishermen gently cast their lines. Then comes the heart of the river's life in the valley where mining, market gardening and farming all went on side by side and where the great house of Cotehele overlooks the fine viaduct of Calstock.

The river's story is one of grandness and suffering and great change, but it remains always the boundary line, the end or beginning of Cornwall, a land of its own.

The Tamar bridges: '. . . the beginning and ending of Cornwall.'

ALSO AVAILABLE

THE CORNISH COUNTRYSIDE
by Sarah Foot

A CORNISH CAMERA
by George Ellis and Sarah Foot

VIEWS OF OLD CORNWALL
by Sarah Foot

VIEWS OF OLD PLYMOUTH
by Sarah Foot

FOLLOWING THE TAMAR
by Sarah Foot

SOMERSET IN THE OLD DAYS
by David Young

NORTH CORNWALL IN THE OLD DAYS
by Joan Rendell

100 YEARS ON BODMIN MOOR
by E. V. Thompson

MOUNT'S BAY
by Douglas Williams

SEA STORIES OF CORNWALL
by Ken Duxbury

SEA STORIES OF DEVON
Introduced by E. V. Thompson

DARTMOOR IN THE OLD DAYS
by James Mildren

STRANGE SOMERSET STORIES
Introduced by David Foot

EXMOOR IN THE OLD DAYS
by Rosemary Anne Lauder

UNKNOWN CORNWALL
by Michael Williams

UNKNOWN DEVON
by Rosemary Anne Lauder,
Michael Williams and Monica Wyatt

AROUND LAND'S END
by Michael Williams

VIEWS OF OLD DEVON
by Rosemary Anne Lauder

AROUND GLORIOUS DEVON
by David Young

LEGENDS OF CORNWALL
by Sally Jones

LEGENDS OF DEVON
by Sally Jones

LEGENDS OF SOMERSET
by Sally Jones

GHOSTS OF CORNWALL
by Peter Underwood

GHOSTS OF DEVON
by Peter Underwood

CURIOSITIES OF CORNWALL
by Michael Williams

CURIOSITIES OF DEVON
by Michael Williams

CORNWALL IN UPROAR
by David Mudd

THE CORNISH EDWARDIANS
by David Mudd

ECCENTRICS IN CORNWALL
by June Lander

KING ARTHUR COUNTRY IN CORNWALL
by Brenda Duxbury, Michael Williams,
Colin Wilson

CASTLES OF CORNWALL
by Mary and Hal Price

STRANGE HAPPENINGS IN CORNWALL
by Michael Williams

We shall be pleased to send you our catalogue giving full details of our growing list of titles for Devon, Cornwall and Somerset and forthcoming publications.

If you have difficulty in obtaining our titles, write direct to Bossiney Books, Land's End, St Teath, Bodmin, Cornwall.